# DINING IN THE

# GREAT

# EMBASSIES

## COOKBOOK

Peggy Whedon
John Kidner

*Edited By*
Blair Brown Hoyt

**PEANUT BUTTER PUBLISHING**
**SEATTLE, WASHINGTON**

10  9  8  7  6  5  4  3  2

© 1987 by Peanut Butter Publishing.
     329 2nd Avenue West
     Seattle, WA  98119
     (206) 281 5965

Assistant Editor:  Sheila Hosner

Produced by Common Sense Publishing.


ISBN  0-89716-147-5

*Dining in the Great Embassies* is dedicated to the ambassadors, their wives, their staffs, and their chefs ..... for their cooperation, good will, and warm encouragement.

# ACKNOWLEDGEMENTS

The wonderful warmth and enthusiasm with which we were received at each embassy made this book possible. Our hosts' patience and good humor were boundless. Very often four or five return visits were necessary before we were sure we understood the recipes and had correctly expressed our hosts' thoughts and feelings. We were honored, as well, to be invited to try the dishes, each prepared by the chef who created them.

Together we say thank you, and "Bon Apetit," from around the world!

Sincerely,

Peggy Whedon and John Kidner

*In addition, grateful thanks, warm affection, and deep appreciation to:*

Elliott Wolf, our good humored and wise publisher from Peanut Butter Publishing.

Tom Tucker, President of Public Affairs Satellite System, Inc. the most understanding "Boss" in the world.

Blair Brown Hoyt, our patient and perspicacious editor.

Sandy and Phil Trupp. Smart, sensitive and stimulating friends and advisors.

# TABLE OF CONTENTS

The glittering parties at Washington, D.C.'s embassies have a world-wide reputation for glamour, intrigue, and marvelous food. Ambassadors, who are members of the world's most exclusive club, are the toast of the town—as are their chefs. Invitations to embassy events are the most sought after in this city of influential entertaining. Everyone wants to know who was where, how they were dressed and what was served.

Guests at embassy parties include the world's great and famous: Prince Charles and Lady Diana, President Ronald Reagan, Prime Minister Margaret Thatcher, Vice President George Bush, Secretary of State George Schultz, Henry Kissinger; stars of the stage, screen and concert halls like Olivia de Haviland, Yves Montand, Robert Redford, Segovia, Issac Stern and Leonard Bernstein.

What do these famous guests eat when they visit the capitol's embassies? How elaborate are the meals? What secrets abide in the preparation and presentation of these elegant dinners?

*DINING IN THE GREAT EMBASSIES* is the first book to peek inside the kitchens, and behind the beautifully decorated banquet halls, to bring you the menus, recipes and backstage preparations for embassy gourmet meals.

The authors visited each embassy individually. They talked with the ambassadors, and their wives—who do most of the social planning. They sat in the kitchens with the chefs and embassy staffs to get the menus, the detailed recipes for each course, and to taste the "piece de resistance." Here are the international recipes, specialized cooking hints and "inside stories" about each country's dining preferences.

Certainly, as one looks at the recipes and mentally prepares them, a single question becomes foremost: "Have they been tried?" In all cases we were assured that each recipe has not only been tried, but savored by heads of state and members of the highest levels of government.

# INTRODUCTION

Not all menus presented here were highlights of formal gatherings. Some were casual lunches. However, all were prepared by the embassy chefs, who kept in mind that their native ingredients are sometimes not available in the United States. Accordingly, many wonderful dishes were thoughtfully adapted, if necessary, to use ingredients available here in international specialty stores. In addition, all oven temperatures are given in Fahrenheit.

Finally, we thought it proper to take a moment in each chapter to tell a little of the origins of each country's native cuisine. Also, we felt a word or two about "His Excellency and Madame" and the embassy chefs' backgrounds, would be in order, as would a description of the magnificent mansions on Embassy Row here in Washington, D.C.

We sincerely hope you find as much pleasure in reading "Dining in the Great Embassies" as you do preparing the exciting dishes in this book.

Peggy Whedon and John Kidner

# DINING IN THE

# GREAT

# EMBASSIES

# THE EMBASSY OF THE
# FEDERATIVE REPUBLIC OF BRAZIL

*Dinner for Six*

### SOUFFLE DE BACALHAU
*(Codfish Souffle)*

### LOMBO DE PORCO COM AMEIXAS
*(Roast Loin of Pork with Prunes)*

### ARROZ BRASILEIRO
*(Brazilian Rice)*

### SALADA COM PALMITO
*(Hearts of Palm Salad)*

### SORVETE DE CAFE
*(Coffee Mousse)*

### DEMITASSE

### COCKTAILS

### BATIDA CAIPIRINHA
*(Rum Drink)*

### PINGA FIZ
*(Batida Rum Drink Variation)*

# FEDERATIVE REPUBLIC OF BRAZIL

Brazil, "The Colossus of the South," occupies nearly half of South America. It is a land of brilliant contrasts: the exotic wildlife of the Amazon rain forest, the endless white sand beaches of Copacabana and Ipanema, the sultry carnival nightlife of Rio de Janeiro, and the perfumed air of Sugar Loaf Mountain laden with the scents of rich coffees and aromatic spices.

The first Europeans to discover Brazil were the Portuguese, in 1500. They set in motion several economic expansion cycles. Their first development in the series was "the Sugar Cane Cycle" in the seventeenth century. This was followed by "the Gold Cycle," "the Diamond Cycle," and in the late nineteenth century, "the Coffee Cycle." The Portuguese and later immigrations of other European and African cultures, along with native groups have all contributed to Brazilian arts and culture as well as to its cuisine.

The Brazilian Embassy in Washington, D.C. is a wonderful, avant-garde, twentieth century structure, a sleek glass building on Massachusetts Avenue. Inside are brilliant modern paintings next to ornately carved wooden chairs from the Portuguese "Colonial period." It is a startling juxtaposition of the old and the new, accurately capturing the intellectual complexity of the brilliant scholar at its helm, Brazilian Ambassador Sergio Correa da Costa.

Ambassador da Costa and his wife, Zazi, have served as diplomats in Ottawa, Los Angeles, Buenos Aires, Rome, London and the United Nations. He speaks five languages, and says of himself: "Politics is my business, but history, especially the nineteenth century, is my pleasure."

The ambassador has written many books on historical subjects: biographies, histories, and literary studies. He is a member of the Brazilian Academy of Letters, Brazil's highest honor for a writer.

His interest in Brazilian history is reflected in the varied and unusual Brazilian dishes prepared for the embassy's dinner parties, which are served in the ambassador's residence, next to the glass-walled chancery. The chef is Italian born, Giuseppe di

Carlo, who has been with Ambassador and Madame da Costa for fifteen years, in London, New York and Washington, D.C.

Parties at the Brazilian Embassy are always festive and music-filled, alive with bossa nova, spicy foods with heavenly sauces, and exotic fruit drinks. The recipes here are for a formal dinner and were personally prepared by Chef Giuseppe di Carlo.

Enjoy a sophisticated, specially prepared dinner with the members of the Embassy of the Federative Republic of Brazil, who would raise their glasses in the toast, "Saude" . . . "To Your Health!"

## SOUFFLE DE BACALHAU
### (Codfish Souffle)

1 pound dried codfish
3 tablespoons butter
1/2 onion, finely chopped
1/4 cup fresh parsley, chopped
1/2 tomato, diced into 1/4 inch cubes
1/2 pound potatoes, boiled
1/2 cup whole milk
3 tablespoons grated yellow Cheddar
4 egg yolks, beaten lightly
4 egg whites, beaten lightly
1/4 cup bread crumbs
tomato sauce, if desired

1) Freshen the fish. Codfish do not always contain the same amount of salt; if they are caught far from land, more salt is used to preserve them. Before cooking, therefore, they must be soaked. Cut the dried fish into large pieces and soak them in cold water for 4 hours, changing the water every hour. Remove the skin and bones. Then refrigerate 12-24 hours until fish tastes fresh.

2) Preheat the oven to 350.

3) After the codfish has been freshened, saute in butter over medium heat in a 10-inch skillet with the onions, parsley, and tomato for 3 to 5 minutes, depending on the size of the codfish pieces.

4) Add the boiled potatoes and mix. Then puree all the ingredients in a food processor or a meat grinder until smooth.

5) Taste for seasoning. Add the milk, 2 tablespoons of the grated cheese, and the beaten egg yolks.

6) Fold in the beaten egg whites.

7) Butter an 8 by 6 inch baking dish and sprinkle with bread crumbs. Pour the pureed mixture into the baking dish and sprinkle with the remaining tablespoon of grated Cheddar. Bake for 30 minutes, until top is browned.

8) Unmold the souffle from the baking dish and serve hot with tomato sauce, if desired.

## LOMBO DE PORCO COM AMEIXAS
### (Roast Loin of Pork with Prunes)

2-pound loin of pork, boned and rolled
1 cup dry white wine
1 tablespoon fresh lemon juice
salt and freshly-ground black pepper, to taste
1 medium clove garlic, crushed
1 large bay leaf
1 1/2 cups sliced onions, or enough to cover bottom of a
    flameproof 8 by 10-inch baking dish
1 tablespoon all-purpose flour
1 pound large prunes, partially cooked and with pits removed

1) Make the marinade: mix 1/2 cup of the wine with the lemon juice, salt, pepper, garlic, and bay leaf. Soak the pork loin overnight.

2) When ready to prepare the roast, preheat the oven to 375.

3) Remove the pork from the marinade, and place it on a bed of sliced onions in a flameproof 8 by 10-inch baking pan. Bake for 40 minutes, or 20 minutes per pound. Baste with half the reserved marinade.

4) When the meat is cooked, remove from the baking pan and drain all the grease. To the remaining drippings, add 1/2 cup water, the remaining half of the marinade, and the remaining 1/2 cup wine.

5) While keeping the roast warm, simmer the sauce. Thicken, if necessary, with a mixture of 1 tablespoon flour and enough cold water to make the liquid the consistency of cream.

6) Pile the pitted prunes in the center of a dish, slice the pork, and arrange the slices around the prunes. Serve the gravy separately. In addition to the Brazilian rice (recipe follows), this recipe may be served with lightly cooked baby carrots and string beans.

## ARROZ BRASILEIRO
### (Brazilian Rice)

*2 cups long-grain rice*
*3 tablespoons unsalted butter*
*1 medium onion, thinly sliced*
*1 tomato, peeled and chopped*
*2 1/4 cups boiling water*
*1/2 teaspoon salt*

1) Wash the rice thoroughly. Melt the butter in a 10-inch skillet.

2) Saute the rice with the onion, stirring gently with a wooden spoon, for about 10 minutes or until the mixture has a swishing sound. This sauteing is crucial; without it the final product will not have the requisite dry texture, in which each grain falls separately from the spoon.

3)' Add the tomatoes, stir, remove from the heat and pour in 2 cups of the boiling water, mixed with the salt.

4) Stir briefly, return to the heat, and bring to a boil. Cover and reduce heat to very low. Cook 20 to 25 minutes, until all the water has evaporated. If the rice is not done to your taste at this point, add the remaining 1/4 cup water and cook until it has evaporated.

5) Remove from heat, uncover, allow steam to evaporate and place in serving dish.

## SALADA COM PALMITO
### (Hearts of Palm Salad)

*6 to 9 hearts of palm, canned*
*6 to 12 lettuce leaves*
*FRENCH DRESSING (see next page)*
*1 bunch watercress, chopped*

1) Cut the palm hearts in half lengthwise, giving each guest two or three pieces.

2) Make a bed of one or two leaves of lettuce on each salad plate.

3) Distribute the hearts of palm among the plates, dress each with FRENCH DRESSING, and sprinkle with the watercress.

# FEDERATIVE REPUBLIC OF BRAZIL

## FRENCH DRESSING

*1/2 cup salad oil*
*2 tablespoons vinegar*
*salt to taste*
*1/2 teaspoon freshly-ground black pepper*
*1/2 clove of garlic, crushed*

Mix the ingredients in a bowl and beat with a fork until thick. If the vinegar is very sharp, add a teaspoon or 2 of cold water, or substitute lemon juice. Do not refrigerate.

## SORVETE DE CAFE
### (Coffee Mousse)

*1 1/2 cups condensed milk*
*1 1/2 cups whole milk*
*1/2 cup Brazilian coffee, or any strong coffee*
*3 egg yolks, beaten lightly*
*2 tablespoons ground, roasted almonds*
*1 1/2 cups heavy whipping cream*
*3 egg whites, beaten until stiff*
*whipped cream and ground coffee beans for garnish*

1) Combine the condensed milk, whole milk, coffee, and egg yolks in a blender, and blend until smooth and creamy.

2) Pour the mixture into a saucepan over low heat; stir constantly until it begins to thicken. Do not boil. Remove from heat. Allow to cool.

3) Add the ground almonds, heavy cream, and egg whites. Fold in thoroughly; refrigerate for at least 2 hours.

4) Serve in parfait glasses, topped with whipped cream and garnished with ground coffee beans.

The Brazilians garnish with ground coffee beans.

## DEMITASSE

*12 tablespoons Brazilian coffee, ground*
*4 1/2 cups cold water*

1) For each serving, use 2 level tablespoons of ground Brazilian coffee and 3/4 cup of cold water.

2) Heat the water to just below the boiling point, about 203 degrees. If you boil the water, the essential oils will be vaporized and the taste will not be at its best.

3) When the water has reached the proper temperature, stir in the measured coffee and remove from the heat.

4) Let the coffee stand 1 minute and stir again, then pour into a filter. Strain directly into a hot coffee pot.

5) The demitasse should be served immediately, very hot, and with plenty of sugar.

## COCKTAILS
### (Each serves one)

### BATIDA CAIPIRINHA
### (Rum Drink)

*1 jigger rum*
*1 teaspoon egg white, beaten until stiff*
*1/4 jigger fresh lemon juice*
*ice as needed*
*1/2 cup sugar, for dipping the rim of the serving glass*

1) Pour all the ingredients, except the sugar, into a cocktail shaker and shake well.

2) Moisten the rim of the glass and dip into sugar. Fill with ice and pour the batida over it. The batida (the word means "beaten" or "whipped") is an entirely original Brazilian drink.

### PINGA FIZ
### (Batida Variation)

*1 jigger rum*
*1/4 jigger fresh lemon juice*
*ice as needed*
*1/2 cup sugar, for dipping the rim of the serving glass*
*club soda*

Mix the rum and lemon juice. Shake well. Pour into a glass which has been dipped in sugar and filled with ice cubes. Add club soda and stir lightly.

THE EMBASSY OF CANADA

*Dinner for Eight*

CREPES WITH NEW BRUNSWICK BLACK STURGEON CAVIAR

PARSLEY SCALLOPS

VEAL PAUPIETTES REGENCE
*(Veal Birds)*

SALADE DE LAITUE
*(Green Salad)*

QUEBEC MAPLE MOUSSE

DEMITASSE

Every few years Washington, D.C.'s skies light up with the advent of diplomatic superstars, and that's just what happened in 1981, when Canadian Ambassador Allan Gotlieb and his wife, Sondra, arrived. Suddenly embassy party invitations were even more eagerly sought after by social lions and media tigers alike. Everyone hoped to be invited to the Canadian Embassy, perchance to sit next to the headliner of the day.

The Canadian Embassy is located in a mansion on Massachusetts Ave. N.W. It was built in 1909 by Clarence Moore and purchased by the Canadian Government in 1927. (Mr. Moore later died in the sinking of the Titanic while transporting hunting dogs from England to the Chevy Chase Hunt Club.)

Some of the outstanding features of the embassy include: its hand-carved library doors; iron balustrades; and beautiful, painted plasterwork on the ceilings and walls. Craftsmen were brought from Italy to create the balustrades and plasterwork. The reception room to the right of the entrance has one of the finest "Adams" ceilings in Washington, D.C. A lovely touch are the embassy's numerous fireplaces which are topped by elegant mirrors inset with Wedgewood medallions.

Over the years, Canada's relations with the United States have grown in many ways. Canada's ambassador in Washington, D.C. oversees the day-to-day diplomatic, trade, cultural, and travel relations, among others, between the two countries. In addition, he supervizes the activities of sixteen consulates throughout the United States.

Sondra Gotlieb has been called a cross between Lucille Ball and Dorothy Parker. She is a humorist, columnist, TV personality, and author. Her books include *Wife of* ... , a popular book about life in Washington D.C.; and two cookbooks. Mrs. Gotlieb is also known for witty, verbal fencing with her French chefs.

Mrs. Gotlieb describes her four-year effort to promote Canadian cuisine in the United States capital as "difficult."

Ottawa's famous turnips never caught on, despite her relentless efforts to focus media attention on them. And Canada's celebrated beef is rarely served to guests because, as Mrs. Gotlieb says, "You have to keep everything light and cholesterol-free or they won't eat it." The prevailing Washington appetite is for white meats such as poultry, fish, or veal.

The recipes which follow are Ambassador and Mrs. Gotlieb's personal favorites. This menu has been served to visiting prime ministers and ministers, and most of the dishes were created by Mrs. Gotlieb. "Fit for an ambassador" is the way Canada's leading United States hostess describes her New Brunswick Black Sturgeon Caviar Crepes and her Quebec Maple Mousse, Canadian specialities now in vogue in Washington,D.C.'s diplomatic circles.

The customary toast before dinner is "Cheers," or "To Your Health," but most Canadians prefer the toast from the Inuit in the far reaches of Northern Canada. It is simply: "Chimo"..."Health."

# CREPES WITH NEW BRUNSWICK BLACK STURGEON CAVIAR

1 cup sifted all-purpose flour
2 eggs
3/4 cup cold milk
salt and white pepper to taste
2 tablespoons melted butter
3 tablespoons parsley, chopped
3 tablespoons chives, chopped
4 tablespoons butter for greasing pan

*For the filling:*

1 level tablespoon caviar per crepe
1 teaspoon chopped onion per crepe
1 tablespoon chopped hard-boiled egg per crepe
1 tablespoon sour cream per crepe
melted butter and lemon juice, mixed to taste

1) Make the crepe batter 3 hours ahead. Put the flour into a bowl; add the eggs, milk, salt and pepper. Mix thoroughly, then strain through a fine sieve. The batter should be light and free of lumps. Add the melted butter, parsley and chives. Let stand at room temperature for 3 hours.

2) Butter a crepe pan or a heavy 4-inch skillet; heat until the butter begins to smoke. Spoon 3 tablespoons of the crepe batter into the pan, tilting until a very thin layer coats the pan.

3) Cook on one side for about 60 seconds, or until golden brown. This will be the outside of the crepe. Flip and cook the other side for 30 seconds.

4) Continue until the crepe batter is used up. Re-butter the pan for each crepe, using about 1/4 tablespoon. The recipe should yield 16 4-inch crepes. They can be served at once or cooled and folded into fours.

5) When ready to serve, place them in a 350-degree oven for about 5 minutes. Serve each guest one or two folded crepes to be unfolded and topped with the caviar, chopped onions, hard-boiled eggs, sour cream, or melted butter and lemon juice.

## PARSLEY SCALLOPS

*3 pounds bay or sea scallops*
*2 cups all-purpose white flour*
*4 tablespoons butter*
*4 tablespoons light vegetable oil*
*1 bunch parsley, finely chopped*
*4 medium-size cloves of garlic, crushed*
*salt and pepper to taste*
*2 medium lemons, cut in wedges*

1) Rinse the scallops in cool water and pat dry. If they are large, cut them into fourths. If they are medium-size, cut in half. If they are small, leave them intact.

2) Place them in a paper bag with the flour and shake until they are well-coated. Shake off the excess flour.

3) Put the butter and oil in a 16-inch Teflon frying pan and melt over medium heat until a test piece of scallop sizzles. Place all the scallops in the pan and cook 5 to 10 minutes or until they begin to brown.

4) Add the chopped parsley and the garlic. Stir skillet contents for about 2 minutes. Remove to a warm serving platter. Add salt and pepper to taste and serve immediately with lemon wedges.

## VEAL PAUPIETTES REGENCE
### (Veal Birds)

2 sweetbreads
1/2 cup white wine vinegar
2 1/4 pounds fresh spinach, or two 10-ounce bags
2 pounds veal scallops (boneless round steaks, 1/2-inch thick)
salt, pepper, and nutmeg to taste
8 strips bacon
2 onions, chopped
2 shallots, chopped
2 carrots, chopped
1 clove of garlic, minced
2 1/2 tablespoons butter
1 tablespoon all-purpose white flour
1/3 cup cognac
2/3 cup dry white wine
1 small bay leaf
4 sprigs fresh thyme
2 tablespoons fresh mint, chopped

1) Preheat the oven to 350.

2) Thoroughly clean and skin the sweetbreads, discarding all soft parts, and put in a pan with cold water to cover. Add the vinegar. Bring to a boil, remove from the heat and let stand until ready to use.

3) Cut off the stems of the spinach, clean it thoroughly, and plunge it into boiling water for 2 minutes. Drain, rinse well in cold water and squeeze to remove excess moisture.

4) Trim any excess fat from the veal and pound the scallops to a 1/4-inch thickness with a wooden mallet, a rolling pin, or the bottom of a heavy pan.

5) Divide the sweetbreads into eight equal portions. Place one portion on each veal scallop, add 2 heaping tablespoons of spinach, and sprinkle with salt, pepper, and nutmeg. Fold the veal over to make a pouch, wrap one strip of bacon around each one and tie firmly with fine string to form a little package.

6) In a flameproof and ovenproof dish, 12 inches in diameter and 4 inches deep, saute the onions, shallots, carrots and garlic in the butter for about 2 minutes or until translucent. Add the veal rolls and brown on all sides. Remove them from the pan, add the flour and cognac, and ignite for an instant. Then add the wine and cook for 2 minutes. Finally, add water to bring the sauce to the consistency of heavy cream. Add the bay leaf and the fresh thyme.

7) Transfer the dish to the preheated oven and bake for 20 to 30 minutes, turning veal occasionally, until tender. Remove the strings, bay leaf, and thyme. Add the mint, simmer for 5 minutes, and serve.

### SALADE DE LAITUE
*(Green Salad)*

12 cups mixed greens (Boston, Bibb, or red leaf lettuce, endive,
    radicchio)
1/3 cup olive oil
1/4 cup corn oil
2 tablespoons white wine vinegar
4 chives, finely chopped
1/4 teaspoon salt
1/4 teaspoon dry mustard
1/8 teaspoon pepper
1 sweet red bell pepper, julienned, for garnish

1) Wash and mix all the greens.

2) Make the vinaigrette: shake the oils, vinegar, and spices in a tightly covered jar. Toss with the greens.

3) Add the red pepper slices just before serving.

## QUEBEC MAPLE MOUSSE

### ALMOND MERINGUE LAYERS

*1 cup white sugar*
*1/3 cup water*
*6 egg whites, room temperature*
*pinch of salt*
*1/4 teaspoon cream of tartar*
*2 1/2 tablespoons white sugar*
*3/4 cup blanched almonds, ground*
*powdered sugar for dusting*

### MAPLE MOUSSE FILLING

*1/4 cup water*
*2 packages unflavored gelatin*
*1 cup maple syrup*
*1/4 cup plus 1 tablespoon brown sugar*
*4 egg whites*
*4 egg yolks*
*pinch of salt*
*2 cups heavy whipping cream*
*marzipan, for garnish*

SPECIAL EQUIPMENT: parchment paper, candy thermometer, pastry bag with a #6 round tip, 10-inch cardboard circle.

1) Cut three 10-inch circles out of parchment paper, then set the circles on a large baking sheet. Or, spread the sheet with melted butter, then sprinkle with flour and draw three 10-inch circles in the flour.

2) Make a sugar syrup by dissolving the cup of white sugar in 1/3 cup of water and bringing to a boil over medium heat. When the liquid turns clear, cover and reduce heat. Simmer while beating the egg whites.

3) Beginning at a slow speed, beat the whites, adding the salt and cream of tartar as they start to foam. Beat faster until stiff peaks form, then beat in the 2 1/2 tablespoons of sugar.

4) Remove the cover from the sugar syrup, turn up the flame, and insert the candy thermometer. Boil rapidly at a temperature of 238 degrees. Once the bubbles begin to thicken, test the syrup by dropping 1/4-teaspoonfuls into ice water. It is ready if it makes a sticky but definable shape between the fingers.

5) Resume beating the egg whites at moderate speed; dribble the boiling syrup into them and continue to beat 8 to 10 minutes, until the mixture cools and forms stiff, glossy peaks. Gently fold in the ground almonds.

6) Preheat the oven to 325.

7) Spoon the meringue into the pastry bag, and pipe it onto the parchment circles, starting in the center and spiraling outward just to the edge. Dust lightly with powdered sugar, then bake until crisp or lightly browned, about 25 minutes. Cool on racks. The meringue layers may be stored in a closely-covered container for up to a week.

8) To make the mousse, dissolve the gelatin in 1/4 cup of warm water in a small bowl. Transfer to the top of a large double boiler. Add the maple syrup and brown sugar and cook over simmering water until the gelatin and sugar are dissolved.

9) Beat the egg yolks in a medium bowl until lemon-colored. Pour in the hot maple mixture a little at a time, beating constantly with an electric mixer or a wire whisk until the liquid has doubled in volume. Cool until it is the consistency of unbeaten egg whites.

10) In a large bowl, whip the cream until stiff.

11)  In a third bowl, whip the egg whites with a pinch of salt until stiff peaks form.

12)  Fold the cooled gelatin syrup into the whipped cream, then fold in the egg whites.

13)  To assemble the dessert, set the 10-inch cardboard circle on a serving plate.  Put a round of meringue on the circle.  Spread it with a layer of maple mousse about 3/4-inch thick.  Add another layer of meringue and another layer of mousse.  Set the last meringue circle on top, and ice the top and sides with the remaining mousse.

14)  Garnish the top with a maple leaf made of marzipan, as they do at the Canadian Embassy; or try colored sugar or slivered almonds

## BEVERAGES

Champagne and/or a good dry white wine are served with the crepes, a white wine with the scallops, a full bodied red wine with the meat, and brandy after dinner with demitasse.

The chef recommends any favorite white, red, and champagne.

# THE EMBASSY OF THE PEOPLE'S REPUBLIC OF CHINA

*Dinner for Six*

### WENCHANG JI
*(Wenchang Cold Chicken)*

### CHAO QUING XIAREN
*(Fried Shrimp with Peas)*

### YU YUO
*(Deep-Fried Fish Toast)*

### CH'AO LUNG HSIA
*(Stir-Fried Lobster)*

### HUNG SHAO NIU JO
*(Chinese Red Beef)*

### DAH MI
*(Rice)*

### NIAN MI
*(Sweet Sticky Rice)*

### SHAO-HSING
*(Wine)*

The Embassy of the People's Republic of China is the most recently established in Washington, D.C. When President Jimmy Carter recognized the People's Republic as the sole government of the Chinese on January 1, 1979, relations between our countries were normalized for the first time since 1949, and the first ambassador, Cai Zhemin, arrived in Washington.

From the outside, the Chinese Embassy is a simple, red brick structure. However, inside the front door one enters a fairyland of exotic artwork. There are floral screens framed with hand-carved black onyx; large glass cases displaying a priceless collection of blue and white thirteenth century Ming vases; and enormous paintings featuring dashing horsemen with swords held aloft, and snow-capped mountains shrouded in clouds.

Chinese lanterns dance around the great reception hall where the new ambassador, His Excellency Han Xu, (who arrived in the spring of 1985), stands to greet his guests. Beyond him, the large ballroom has been turned into a dining room with round tables, seating ten each. Cold appetizers are waiting: large shrimp, marinated beef or ham, and carrots carved into pagoda shapes or peacock designs.

The exotic banquets served here are a tremendous challenge to the chef and his many assistants. They require techniques far more sophisticated than those of the ordinary Chinese cook, and the ingredients used are rare and expensive: duck webs in oyster sauce; braised chicken feet with wild herbs; turtle; shark's-fin soup; steamed carp; and roast sparrow.

Embassy cuisine features the best of Cantonese, Szechuan, Shanghai and Beijing cooking. The Canton province, in Southern China, is noted for its pastries and for *dim sum*, which is delicacies such as pork buns, shrimp toasts, spring rolls and steamed beef balls. Diners choose from an assortment of *dim sum* on carts, wheeled directly from the kitchen to the table .

Northern or Beijing cooking developed from the Moslem cooking of Inner Mongolia, with highly seasoned barbeques.

Peking roast duck, shark's-fin soup, and Mongolian hot-pot are all Beijing specialities.

Szechuan and Hunan cooking is hot and peppery, featuring chilis, pimentos, red peppers, and spicy peanut sauces. The Chinese believe that spices are necessary cooking ingredients, especially in hotter climates, and "to gasp is to enjoy."

On the other hand, Shanghai is a city that plays it cool. It is expected to produce 2,500 tons of ice cream this summer, fifty-eight percent more than last year. Residents of China's biggest city consume over 100 tons of ice cream on a summer day. Shanghai food is sweet with more sugar and dark soy sauce. Noodles and vegetables are popular, but the coastal location makes seafood, prawns, crab, and saltwater fish Shanghai specialties.

The seating for a formal Chinese dinner, whether in Washington, D.C. or in Beijing, dates back to ancient times when the War Lords might make unexpected entrances. The guests of honor face the door, and the host and hostess sit opposite,with their backs to the door.

The regional specialties are placed on a lazy susan in the center of each dining table. As the dishes rotate, each guest helps himself. *Shao-Hsing* wine is serve throughout the meal. The first toast by the standing host is to the guest of honor. Everyone joins in. This is followed by a complimentary introduction and a toast to each couple. Then the guests of honor toast the host and hostess, and, again, all join in. The guests are then free to toast whomever they please and as often as they wish, drinking the popular liquor *moutai*. Boisterous guests have been known to upend their glasses on their heads to prove that they have drunk all the contents. When the host and hostess rise to leave the party is over.

The standard toast, "Gam Bei," literally means "Bottoms Up."

## WENCHANG JI
### (Wenchang Cold Chicken)

*2-pound chicken*
*1/2 pound chicken livers*
*1/4 pound cooked lean ham*
*5 tablespoons vegetable oil, for deep frying*
*1 cup fresh string beans, stems and strings removed*
*1/4 teaspoon salt*
*1 cup chicken stock or bouillon*
*1/4 teaspoon cornstarch, mixed with 3 teaspoons cold water*
*1/2 teaspoon rice wine or sherry*

1) To prepare the chicken, rinse it well, place it in a pot and cover it with boiling water. Bring the water to a boil again, reduce heat, and simmer for about 15 minutes. To keep it at the same temperature throughout, pick it up three or four times during this process and empty the water from its cavity. When it is done, the bones should be easy to remove. Drain the chicken, then skin it and bone it. Cut the meat into 24 diamond-shaped pieces, 1 by 1 inch.

2) To prepare the livers, boil a cup of water, add 1/4 teaspoon of salt, and put in the chicken livers. Blanche them, then remove the pan from the heat and leave the livers in the water until it is lukewarm. If they have not yet changed color, repeat the process. When done, cut the livers into 24 diamond-shaped pieces of the same dimensions as the chicken.

3) To prepare the ham, cut it into 24 pieces like those of the other meats.

*THE PEOPLE'S REPUBLIC OF CHINA*

4) To arrange the platter, make three rows of the sliced meats. Each row should have an equal number of pieces of each meat, arranged in sequence: chicken, then liver, then ham. Keep the rows about 3/4 of an inch apart.

5) To prepare the string beans, heat 4 teaspoons of the oil in an 8-inch skillet at medium heat. When the oil is hot, add the string beans, the salt, and 1/2 cup of hot water. Stir-fry for 2 minutes, remove the beans, and pour off the liquid. Heat another 4 teaspoons of oil and fry the beans again. Add 6 teaspoons of the stock and 2 teaspoons of the cornstarch solution. Stir-fry for 45 seconds. Again remove the beans and discard the liquid.

6) Add the beans to the meat platter, arranging them in equal numbers in the spaces left between rows, and on the outside of the upper and lower rows.

7) To make the sauce, heat the remaining oil in the skillet and add the remaining stock and the rice wine or sherry. Slowly stir in the remaining 1 teaspoon of cornstarch solution. Mix well, pour over the meats, and serve.

## CHAO QUING XIAREN
### (Fried Shrimp with Peas)

*2 tablespoons powdered ginger*
*4 teaspoons cornstarch*
*2 teaspoons salt*
*2 egg whites*
*1 1/2 pounds medium-size shrimp, peeled, cleaned, patted dry*
*4 cups vegetable oil*
*4 teaspoons minced scallions*
*4 teaspoons minced ginger root*
*6 tablespoons fresh or canned peas*
*4 teaspoons rice wine or sherry*
*1/2 teaspoon wine vinegar*
*1 bunch fresh parsley, for garnish*

1) Mix the powdered ginger with 2 tablespoons of water. Set aside.

2) Mix the cornstarch with 4 teaspoons of water. Set aside.

3) Mix half the salt, the egg white, and the cornstarch solution in a medium bowl and put in the shrimp. Stir to coat thoroughly.

4) Pour the vegetable oil into a heavy skillet and bring to a boil over a high heat, then reduce to a medium heat. Using a large fork or a slotted spoon, drop four to six of the coated shrimp into the oil. Remove them as they begin to float.

5) When all the shrimp are cooked, pour off the oil. Using the same skillet (do not clean it) over a high heat, fry the scallions and ginger root for no more than 5 seconds. Now add the shrimp, the peas, the wine, the powdered ginger solution, the vinegar, and the remaining salt. Stir-fry for no more than 8 seconds. Remove and serve on a platter, garnished with parsley.

## YU YUO
### (Deep-Fried Fish Toast)

*6 slices white bread*
*8 ounces boned white fish*
*1 egg, beaten lightly*
*2 1/2 tablespoons cornstarch*
*1/4 teaspoon salt*
*1/4 teaspoon freshly-ground pepper*
*12 thin slices unsalty ham, about the size of 1/2 slice of bread*
*2 cups oil for deep frying*
*12 coriander leaves, for garnish*

1) Cut each slice of bread in half and set pieces aside.

2) In a skillet, poach the fish for a few minutes in water to give it a firm texture.

3) In a large bowl mash the cooked fish with a fork. When the fish is of an even consistency, add the egg, cornstarch, salt, pepper, and a teaspoon of cool water. Mix the ingredients thoroughly.

4) Spread equal portions of this mixture onto the half slices of bread. Top each with a piece of ham; press firmly in place.

5) Heat the oil over a high heat, and when it begins to smoke, drop in each of the fish breads and cook until golden brown.

6) Place on a warm serving dish and garnish with coriander leaves.

### CH'AO LUNG HSIA
### (Stir-Fried Lobster)

*2 2-pound lobsters*
*1 teaspoon salt*
*1 egg white, lightly beaten*
*1/2 tablespoon cornstarch*
*4 cups oil*
*3 tablespoons tomato sauce*
*1 tablespoon sugar*
*1/2 tablespoon vinegar*
*2 tablespoons cornstarch, dissolved in 2 tablespoons water*
*1/2 tablespoon sesame oil*
*1/2 tablespoon curry powder*
*1/4 cup chicken broth*
*1/2 teaspoon salt*

1) Cook the lobsters by immersing them in a large pot of boiling water, letting the water return to the boil, and simmering for 10 minutes. Let them cool enough to handle.

2) Remove the meat from the lobsters and cut it into half-inch squares. Combine the salt, beaten egg white, and 1/2 tablespoon cornstarch, and coat the lobster pieces with this mixture.

3) Heat the oil in a 12-inch skillet or a wok. When it reaches 325 degrees and is smoking, add the lobster pieces and stir–fry for 40 seconds. Remove the lobster, drain, and divide into two batches—one will be cooked in tomato sauce and the other in curry sauce. Pour off the oil, reserving 2 tablespoons.

4) Heat 1 tablespoon of the reserved oil in the skillet until it smokes. Add the tomato sauce and cook, stirring, for a second. Add the sugar, the vinegar, and 1/2 cup of water. When these are mixed, put in one batch of the lobster pieces. Stir-fry for another second. Remove from heat and stir in half of the cornstarch-water solution. When all the ingredients are well mixed, add the sesame oil, toss lightly, and remove to a serving plate.

5) Heat the other tablespoon of oil. Add the curry powder and stir-fry for a few seconds. Add the salt and chicken broth. When mixed, put in the other half of the lobster pieces. After 1 second, stir in the rest of the cornstarch solution. When the lobster is covered with the sauce, remove to a serving plate.

## HUNG SHAO NIU JO
### (Chinese Red Beef)

2 pounds beef round
1 1/2 cups water
2 tablespoons white wine
1/4 cup soy sauce
1 tablespoon sugar
4 tablespoons vegetable oil
1 green onion, halved lengthwise
1 clove of garlic, halved
1 teaspoon freshly-ground pepper
4 sprigs of coriander or fresh parsley, for garnish
4 tablespoons toasted sesame seed, for garnish

1) Mix the water, wine, soy sauce and sugar; stir well and set aside.

2) Remove the fat from the beef and cut the beef into 1 to 1 1/2-inch cubes. In a 12-inch skillet, heat 2 tablespoons of the oil. Stir-fry half the beef cubes 2 to 2 1/2 minutes. When the cubes are browned on all sides, place them in a 3-quart sauce pan. Stir-fry the remaining beef cubes in the same fashion, in the remaining oil.

3) Pour the sauce over the beef and add the ginger, green onion, garlic, and pepper. Bring to a boil, then reduce the heat and simmer until the beef is tender, about an hour.

4) Transfer the beef to a serving platter, garnish with coriander or parsley and sesame seeds, and serve with hot cooked Chinese noodles.

## DAH MI
### (Rice)

*2 cups uncooked rice*
*3 cups water*

1) Wash and drain the rice.  Place it in an uncovered saucepan and add 3 cups of water.

2) Over medium heat, boil the rice until most of the water is absorbed, from 3 to 5 minutes.

3) Reduce the heat to very low, cover the saucepan, and cook for another 15 minutes. Use a fork to fluff rice before serving.

## NIAN MI
### (Sweet Sticky Rice)

*3 cups sticky or glutinous rice, available in Chinese food stores*
*3 cups water*
*2 1/2 tablespoons shortening*
*4 tablespoons sugar*
*candied nuts, dates, raisins, candied orange peel and lotus seed*
*1 cup red bean paste, available in Chinese food stores*

*SYRUP:*

*1 cup water*
*3 tablespoons sugar*
*4 teaspoons cornstarch*

1) Wash the rice and stir it into the water.  Follow the directions on the box for cooking the rice.

# THE PEOPLE'S REPUBLIC OF CHINA

2) Mix 2 tablespoons of the shortening and the sugar into the cooked rice.

3) Grease an 8-inch diameter mold or bowl with the remaining shortening.  On the bottom of the mold, arrange the candied ingredients into a design.

4) Carefully spread 2/3 of the rice mixture over the candied ingredients.  Spread the bean paste onto this and cover it with the rest of the rice.

5) Gently flatten the contents of the mold and steam for 2 hours. Unmold onto a deep platter.

6) Make the syrup by boiling the water, sugar, and cornstarch together.  Pour this over the dessert and serve hot with Sesame Sweet Cakes, which can be purchased in any gourmet or Chinese food store.

# THE EMBASSY OF THE
# THE KINGDOM OF DENMARK

*Dinner for Ten*

## MOUSSE AF LAKS SERVERET MED MARINEREDE ASPARAGES
*(Salmon Mousse with Marinated Asparagus and Green Sauce)*

## KAMMUSLINGER I ROSETTE PA SPINAT SERVERET MED SAUCE BEURRE BLANC
*(Rosette of Sea Scallops on
Spinach Bed with Sauce Beurre Blanc)*

## KALVEFILET FARSERET MED VAGTLER, ARSTIDENS GRONSAGER, OSTERS HAT
## RASTEGTE KARTOFLER MED TIMIAN
*(Roast Tenderloin of Veal Stuffed with Breast of Quail)*
*(Potatoes with Thyme)*

## PARFAIT ISKAGE MED MANDLER OG CHOKOLADE
*(Parfait Cake with Almonds and Chocolate)*

## WINES

The Royal Danish Ambassador, His Excellency Eigil Jorgensen, and his wife, Madame Alice Jorgensen, have presided over the Embassy of the Kingdom of Denmark in Washington, D.C. for more than two years. The ambassador's service to his country includes ten years as undersecretary of state, and eight years in the prime minister's office. He also served as ambassador to Bonn and Paris.

Denmark is ranked by a University of Pennsylvania study as first among 107 countries as: "the best place in the world to live." The warm, open friendliness of the Danes and the country's proximity to the sea are major reasons. Denmark comprises five hundred islands, one hundred of which are inhabited by the five million Danes. Nobody lives more than forty-five miles from a beach.

Since the dawn of their Viking history, Danish fishermen have taken oysters, salmon, fresh fish, eels, and mussels from the sea. This traditional harvest accounts for the great variety of superbly-prepared fresh and smoked fish that make up no small part of the Danes' daily diet.

Danish meals are an occasion for joy and celebration among friends. Homes often have a very large family room, the alrum, where everyone can gather for homework, hobbies, reading, cooking, and dining. The space for this great room is made available by reducing the size of the bedrooms and parlor.

The open-faced sandwich, a complete meal arranged on dark bread is a Danish tradition, as is the *smorgaasbord*, the "big cold table," which, despite its name, often includes hot dishes among its ten to fifty delicacies. Preparing an outstanding *smorgaasbord* requires several years of training in cooking and arranging.

The embassy's chef, Michael Madson, has had just such experience: five years at La Cocotte in Copenhagen, and several months as fish chef at the King Frederik Hotel, also in the capital. He has been with the Jorgensens since their arrival here, and shares their respect for the old Danish traditions. Meals at the embassy are marked by careful attention to table settings, often inspired by the seasons of the year. The long dark winter is perfect for candlelight and a frosty-white tablecloth. Spring means fresh green leaves and a pink or yellow tablecloth. Summer features an endless variety of lovely flowers and delicious fruits, and fall offers colored leaves and red berries to highlight the decor.

Whether *smorgaasbord*, daily repast, or formal dinner, each meal is accompanied by fine wines from the vineyard of the Danish Consul in Bordeaux. Other drinks include well-chilled beer (the national beverage, brewed in Denmark since 1,000 B.C.) and world-famous *aquavit*–"Water of Life".

When drinking aquavit, lift your glass in salute, not slightly, and say "Skaal!" Then down the contents in a gulp. Put the glass down and say, "Ah."

It is customary for the host to drink first. After the *aquavit* is poured the host will look the guest straight in the eye as he raises his glass and drinks to his or her health.

The following recipes were prepared by Chef Michael Madson for a very important dinner for the Prime Minister of Denmark, Paul Schlucter, Vice President of the United States, George Bush, and Secretary of Defense, Caspar W. Weinberger.

Ambassador and Mrs. Jorgensen invite you to prepare and savor some of their favorite dishes.

## MOUSSE AF LAKS SERVERET MED MARINEREDE ASPARAGES
### (Salmon Mousse with Marinated Asparagus and Green Sauce)

*1 pound fresh salmon, skinned and boned*
*3 eggs*
*1 pint whipping cream*
*salt and pepper to taste*
*45 stalks asparagus*
*10 romaine lettuce leaves*
*GREEN SAUCE (see following page)*

1)  Preheat the oven to 350.

2)  Steam five asparagus spears in boiling water for 5 minutes.

3) Cut the salmon into 1/2-inch cubes.  Chop in the food processor for 1 minute.  Add the eggs and process again for 45 seconds.

4) Add the whipping cream using the on/off switch on the food processor for 3 or 4 minutes until it reaches the consistency of a thick whipped mousse. Add salt and pepper to taste.

5) Butter a 12-inch loaf pan (it should hold one quart).  Spread a one-inch layer of the mousse in the bottom.  Place the steamed asparagus on top, then cover with the remaining mousse. Cover with buttered aluminum foil.

6) Place the pan in a *bain-marie* (a larger, deeper pan with an inch of water in it) and bake for 1 hour.

7) Remove from the oven and chill for at least 5 hours before serving.

8) Poach the remaining asparagus in lightly salted water for 5 minutes and chill.

9) Blanch the romaine lettuce, chill in ice water, and dry with paper towels.

10) Place four asparagus spears on each lettuce leaf. Pour a tablespoon of GREEN SAUCE on, and wrap the lettuce around the asparagus. Chill.

11) To serve, place a 3/4-inch slice of mousse and an asparagus roll on each plate. Ladle a spoonful of GREEN SAUCE over them.

### GREEN SAUCE

*1 bunch parsley*
*1 bunch watercress*
*1 bunch dill*
*4 shallots*
*1 clove of garlic*
*3 hard boiled eggs*
*5 ounces olive oil*
*1 ounce vinegar*
*1 tablespoon mustard*
*salt and pepper to taste*

Chop the first six ingredients finely and mix with the olive oil, the vinegar, the mustard, and the salt and pepper.

## KAMMUSLINGER I ROSETTE PA SPINAT SEVERET MED SAUCE BEURRE BLANC
### (Rosette of Sea Scallops on Spinach Bed with Sauce Beurre Blanc)

*30 large fresh sea scallops, cleaned and cut into 3 slices each*
*1/4 cup melted butter*
*salt and pepper to taste*
*paprika to taste*
*4 pounds fresh spinach*
*1/2 cup olive oil*
*BEURRE BLANC (see following page)*

1) Preheat the broiler.

2) In a 12 by 14-inch baking pan, make 10 rosettes (circles of overlapping scallop slices), using nine slices in each. Brush with a little melted butter, sprinkle with the salt, pepper and paprika, and broil 4 inches from the flame for approximately 5 minutes.

3) Rinse and shred the spinach. Marinate for 3 minutes in the olive oil, toss well, and arrange on luncheon plates. Place one rosette on each bed of spinach and cover with BEURRE BLANC.

### BEURRE BLANC

4 shallots, finely chopped
1 clove of garlic, minced
12 tablespoons unsalted butter
3 ounces white wine
2 cups chicken broth
1 bunch parsley, finely chopped
salt and pepper to taste

Saute the shallots and garlic in a little of the butter. Add the wine and reduce by half. Add the broth and again reduce by half. With the sauce boiling, stir in the rest of the butter a little at a time until it thickens. Complete with the parsley and salt and pepper.

## KALVEFILET FARSERET MED VAGTLER, ARSTIDENS GRONSAGER, OSTERS HAT
## RASTEGTE KARTOFLER MED TIMIAN
(Roast Tenderloin of Veal Stuffed with Breast of Quail)
(Potatoes with Thyme)

5 quails
2 tablespoons unsalted butter
1 2-pound tenderloin of veal, skinned and cleaned
salt and pepper

SAUCE:

Bones and thighs of 5 quails
1 carrot, sliced
1 leek, sliced
1 celery stalk, sliced
1 quart chicken stock
1 tablespoon cornstarch dissolved in 1 tablespoon cold water
1 pound cleaned oyster mushrooms, or any mushroom
8 tablespoons unsalted butter
1 cup heavy cream

1) Skin and bone the breasts of quail, reserving the bones and thighs for the sauce.  Saute for 2 or 3 minutes in 2 tablespoons butter.  Then chill.

2) Preheat the oven to 400.

3) With a sharp filet knife, cut an opening through the veal loin lengthwise, creating a small hole.  Do not pierce the sides.

4) Carefully insert the quail breasts into the veal loin, two from one end and three from the other. Tie the roast to keep the quail pieces from slipping out.

5) Season to taste and roast until a golden brown, about 1 1/4 hours, or until a meat thermometer reads 180. Baste once, halfway through the cooking, with the roast drippings. Let stand for 10 minutes before slicing.

6) To make the sauce, brown the quail bones and thighs in a large saucepan. Add the carrot, leek, celery, and chicken broth. Boil on low heat for 15 minutes. Strain. Thicken the sauce with the cornstarch/water solution.

7) Rinse the mushrooms, and then saute them in the butter for 10 minutes at medium heat in a 10-inch saucepan.

8) Add the quail sauce and the cream. Boil for 5 minutes. Arrange the sliced roast on a platter, and serve it with the sauce and potatoes (see below).

## RASTEGTE KARTOFLER MED TIMIAN
### (Potatoes with Thyme)

*2 pounds medium-size red potatoes*
*4 tablespoons unsalted butter*
*salt and pepper to taste*
*1 bunch fresh thyme, washed and trimmed*

1) Preheat oven to the 350.

2) Peel the potatoes and slice 1/4 inch thick. Wash, and dry with paper towels.

3) Melt the butter in a 12-inch flameproof and ovenproof pan. Saute the potatoes for 3 to 5 minutes. Add the salt, pepper, and thyme.

4) Transfer the pan to the oven. Bake for 30 minutes.

This dish is served with fresh vegetables in season

### PARFAIT ISKAGE MED MANDLER OG CHOKOLADE
(Parfait Cake with Almonds and Chocolate)

*1 pound sugar*
*2 cups water*
*16 egg yolks*
*1/2 pound lightly toasted almonds, chopped*
*1/2 pound semisweet chocolate, coarsely chopped*
*4 cups whipped cream, slightly sweetened*
*sliced almonds, for garnish*

1) Boil the sugar and water until it reaches the syrup stage (about 15 minutes over medium heat).

2) Add the egg yolks to the boiling syrup while beating vigorously. Remove the mixture from the heat and continue beating until it is cool and thick.

3) Divide the syrup into two portions. Add the almonds to one portion and pour into a springform pan 10 inches diameter and 4 to 6 inches deep. Freeze for 1 hour.

4) Add the chocolate to the other portion of the syrup. Pour the mixture into the springform pan and freeze again.

5) When the cake is frozen, remove it from the pan; top with the whipped cream and sprinkle with the sliced almonds.

# THE EMBASSY OF THE
# ARAB REPUBLIC OF EGYPT

*Dinner for Six*

## BABA GHANNOOJ
*(Eggplant Dip)*

## TAGIN OF GAMBARY
*(Special Dish with Shrimp)*

## CHIRKASIA
*(Chicken, Rice, and Nut Sauce)*

## TOSSED GREEN SALAD

## OM ALY
*(Mother of Aly Dessert)*

## COFFEE AND MINTS

The Embassy of the Arab Republic of Egypt is a large, four-story white mansion that dominates a corner of Massachusetts Avenue on Washington, D.C.'s Embassy Row. Its white columns, balconies, terraces, and winged gargoyles would also fit in perfectly on the banks of the Nile–the Sahara, pyramids, sphinx, and Temples of Karnak forming the background.

Once inside the heavy carved doors, the guest finds himself in a thirty-foot wide, red-carpeted hallway ending in a broad winding stairway to the second floor. The entrance hall is flanked by two reception rooms furnished with gold-filigreed tables, chairs, statues and *objets d'art* of ancient Egypt.

Ambassador and Madame El Sayed Abdel Raouf El Reedy entertain frequently, holding receptions for 100 people or more as well as intimate dinner parties for twenty-four to thirty guests. Seating at the dinners is around a large, intricately-carved mahogany table given to the Embassy by King Faud, father of King Farouk.

Madame El Reedy, the raven-haired, chic wife of the ambassador, personally supervises all the menus. They are prepared by Chef Mahmoud, who has been with the embassy for sixteen years. As Madame El Reedy describes his cooking, she also praises his helpfulness when they first arrived in Washington after serving in Pakistan, Geneva and Cairo. Of course, Chef Mahmoud was on hand for Madame El Reedy's welcoming dinner for Egypt's President Hosni Mubarak, held at the embassy in March of 1985.

Like most Egyptian hosts, Madame El Reedy takes entertaining and food preparation seriously. This is understandable, since the cuisine, handed down through centuries, mixes the best of many countries–indeed, of whole civilizations. History was born here, and with it, the cooking traditions of the ancient world. Garlic was worshipped as a god by the Egyptians, and the recipe for making beer was found on a 6,000-year-old papyrus.

Madame El Reedy prefers to serve Egyptian food at her dinner parties. Her selected appetizers might be vine leaves with cucumber, yogurt, and mint—or *baba ghannooj*, an eggplant dip. The main course often is *tagin of gambary*, a special dish with shrimp; and *chirkasia*, a special chicken and rice dish with a pecan sauce. These exotic and typically Egyptian entrees would be followed by a tossed green salad with a simple oil-and-vinegar dressing. To complete the feast, there would be hot *Om Aly*, a rich layered pastry with raisins and nuts–a specialty so old that no one today knows who "Aly" was. These delights are served in the large, panelled dining room on tables elegantly decorated with roses and chrysanthemums, and set with gold-edged dishes and gold candelabra. After dinner, guests retire to the comfortable drawing room for coffee and mints.

The recipes for these Middle Eastern specialities are supplied by Madame El Reedy and Chef Mahmoud. Try them and dream of the sun-drenched Sahara, the giant temples and dazzling statues of Luxor, and the white sails of the feluccas floating serenely on the Nile in the land of the ancient Pharoahs.

### BABA GHANNOOJ
(Eggplant Dip)

*1 1-pound eggplant*
*1 clove of garlic*
*1 small onion, chopped*
*1/4 cup fresh lemon juice*
*1 1/2 teaspoon olive oil*
*1 teaspoon salt*
*carrot and celery strips for dipping*

1) Preheat the oven to 400.

2) Prick the eggplant several times with a fork and place in the oven for about 40 minutes, or until tender. Let cool.

3) Peel the eggplant, and cut into chunks. Put it into a blender with the garlic, lemon juice, olive oil, and salt; process at medium or high speed until smooth. Serve with the vegetable strips for dipping.

## TAGIN OF GAMBARY
### (Special Dish with Shrimp)

*30-36 cleaned and deveined shrimp (5 or 6 for each diner)*
*4 tablespoons corn oil*
*1 medium onion, chopped*
*2 cloves garlic, finely chopped*
*2 stalks celery, chopped*
*1 teaspoon parsley, chopped*
*2 medium-size tomatos, diced*
*juice of 2 limes*
*1 cup tomato juice*
*1 tomato, sliced*
*1 lime, sliced*

1) Preheat the oven to 350.

2) Heat the oil in a 12-inch pan. Fry the onions until golden. Add the garlic, celery, parsley, diced tomatoes, lime juice, and tomato juice. Let the mixture boil for 2 minutes.

3) Arrange the shrimp in one layer in a baking dish. Pour the sauce over them and top with the tomato and lime slices.

4) Place in the oven and bake for 30 minutes or until the top becomes golden and crisp.

5) Serve with white rice.

### CHIRKASIA
( Chicken, Rice, and Nut Sauce)

6 *chicken breasts*
8 *cups water*
1 *medium-size onion, chopped*
1 *bay leaf*
*salt and pepper to taste*
1 *or 2 cardamom seeds*
2 *cups short-grain white rice*
5 *cups chicken broth*

*SAUCE:*

2 *tablespoons margarine or butter*
2 *cloves garlic, finely minced*
1 *teaspoon paprika*
6 *slices white bread, crusts removed, dampened in water*
1 1/2 *pounds pecans, shelled*
2 *cups chicken broth*

1)  Boil the chicken breasts in the water with the chopped onion, bay leaf, salt, pepper and cardamom seed.  When they are tender (in about 45 minutes), remove them and keep them warm.

2)  Cook the rice in the chicken broth for at least 30 minutes so that it is well cooked and slightly wet.

3) To make the sauce, fry the garlic in the margarine until golden brown.  In a blender mix the garlic, paprika, bread, pecans, and chicken broth.  Blend until smooth.  Boil the sauce at medium heat for 1 minute.

4) To serve, arrange the rice around the outside rim of a large round serving dish. Place the chicken breasts on top of the rice around the platter. Place the pecan sauce in a round bowl in the center of the platter, and serve immediately. Each guest helps himself to rice, chicken and pecan sauce.

### TOSSED GREEN SALAD

*1 head of romaine*
*3 tomatoes, quartered*
*1 cucumber, sliced very thin*
*2 green peppers, sliced horizontally very thin*
*1 bunch watercress, chopped coarsely*

Mix all ingredients; add oil, vinegar, salt, and pepper to taste.

# ARAB REPUBLIC OF EGYPT

## OM ALY
### (Mother of Aly Dessert)

*12 ounces dried white raisins*
*2 packages frozen puff pastry (available in supermarkets)*
*1 tablespoon unsalted butter*
*1 pound mixed nuts (hazelnuts, almonds, pecans), roasted and*
   *chopped*
*2 cups milk*
*12 tablespoons brown sugar*
*1 vanilla pod*
*1 cup heavy whipping cream*
*3 tablespoons pistachios, roasted and chopped*

1)  Preheat the oven to 375.

2)  Soak the raisins in hot water for 1 hour.

3)  Brush the puff pastry with the butter and bake on large cookie sheets until golden–about 20 minutes.   Change the oven temperature to 350.

4) Break the baked pastry into 3-inch squares.   In a 12-inch souffle dish, place a layer of pastry pieces, then a layer of nuts, then a layer of raisins.  Alternate layers of the pastry, the nuts, and the raisins, finishing with the nuts.

5) Heat the milk with the sugar, the vanilla pod and the cream. Pour the hot liquid over the layers in the dish and bake for 40 minutes, until the top layer of nuts, and the puff pastry beneath, are crisp and golden brown.

6) Before serving, sprinkle the dessert with the pistachios. Serve very hot.

# THE EMBASSY OF FRANCE

*Luncheon for Four*

## SALADE DE LANGOUSTINES AUX TRUFFLES
*(Salad of Langoustines and Truffles)*

## CAILLES AUX RIS DE VEAU ET AUX CEPES
*(Quail Stuffed with Sweetbreads and Cepes)*

## POMMES PAILLASON
*(Straw Potatoes)*

## SALADE

## FROMAGE
*(Cheese)*

## CHARLOTTE AUX FRAMBOISES
*(Vanilla Cream with Raspberry Sauce)*

## WINES

*MEURSAULT 1982*
*CHATEAU LATOUR 1975*

# FRANCE

Dining at the Embassy of the French Republic is the ultimate experience in haute cuisine. The executive chef, Francis Layrle, who was trained in the Pyrenees, would not hesitate to fly in frogs' legs from Paris and black truffles from Perigord for a special luncheon. In culinary affairs he always aims for excellence and elegance; both are evident in his extraordinary food.

The chef works closely with Madame Helene de Margerie, the svelte and pretty wife of the French Ambassador, Emmanuel de Margerie. The de Margeries have represented their country for many years, setting exquisite tables in the U.S.S.R., Spain, Britain, and Canada before coming to the U.S.A. They routinely entertain dignitaries and statesmen for luncheon or dinner up to six times a week. The guests may number from six to a hundred.

While both the ambassador and his wife sample each new dish before it's served, the menus reflect Madame de Margerie's personal tastes. She selects recipes from her family's dinners in Paris, from the formal dinners served in world capitals, and from the culinary skills of Chef Layrle. She speaks of the period "between the wars" as a time of great change in French cuisine.

"I remember when I was a young girl," she reminisces, "how meals with guests were celebrations. For dinner there would be soup. After that there would be fish and meat courses: beef, lamb, pork...then cold chicken or cold duck would be served with the salad. Next came the vegetables.

"Mind you, each was a separate course. Between each of them the table would be cleared. I can still see the great plate of asparagus. They were so tender. Not like the sticks of wood you sometimes get now.

"After the vegetables there would be cheese followed by fruit. My father was traditional. He thought it not quite right to leave a magnificent table with the taste of Camembert clinging to one's palate. Then the meal would close with a dessert.

"And the wines! White wine or white burgundy with the

fish, and red wine with the meat and chicken. A third wine, sauterne, could be served with the dessert.

"After the dinner, we would sometimes sit at the table and chat, savoring champagne and petit fours. And when dinner was over everybody would go to the dining room for coffee and cognac.

"Those were the times when the cuisine was so much different. The food was rich, very plentiful and many herbs were used.

"Of course, in those times there was NEVER any alcohol served before the meal. Guests would arrive just a few minutes before dinner, talk a bit, then retire to the dining room. Dinner was such a gracious affair and lasted a long time.

"Yes indeed, it was a celebration."

Both Madame de Margerie and Chef Layrle believe that preparing, serving, and savoring these French menus is a delightful experience and an exhibit of culinary art. The artist's palette: langoustine, quail, truffles, and cepes. The canvas: an exquisitely-set table with flowers, candles, silverware, and four sparkling glasses at each place. Imagine yourself in a grand dining room with gold toile panels and mirrored walls, overlooking a terrace, garden, and pool. Madame de Margerie and Chef Layrle wish you "bon appetit."

## SALADE DE LANGOUSTINES AUX TRUFFLES
### (Salad of Langoustine and Truffles)

*2 pounds lobster meat (small spiny lobsters are closest to angoustines)*
*1 black truffle, medium size, or one 1-ounce can of truffles*
*1/2 cup olive oil*
*1 tablespoon white wine vinegar*
*1/2 teaspoon chives, finely chopped*
*1/4 teaspoon salt*
*1/4 teaspoon pepper*
*1 head red-leaf lettuce*
*12 leaves purslane or any dark green lettuce*
*1 ripe tomato, sliced*

1) If you are using a fresh truffle, peel off the thin outer skin with a sharp kitchen knife, then wash it. Simmer it in water to cover for a minute, then let it cool. Reserve the liquid. Chop the truffle very finely. If you are using canned truffles, chop them very finely and reserve the liquid.

2) To make the vinaigrette, mix the oil and vinegar well and whisk in the truffle liquid. Add the chives, salt, and pepper.

3) Poach the lobsters (about 12 will yield 2 pounds of meat) for 1 minute in water to cover. Let them cool, then remove the shells and cut the meat into bite-size chunks. Chill them.

4) Make a bed of red-leaf lettuce on a serving platter. Arrange the chilled lobster meat on top of the lettuce. Sprinkle the chopped truffles onto the lobster meat. Around the edge of the platter, arrange the purslane and the sliced tomato.

5) Dress the salad with the vinaigrette just before serving.

## CAILLES AUX RIS DE VEAU ET AUX CEPES
(Quail Stuffed with Sweetbreads and Cepes)

*4 domestic quails*
*2 tablespoons plus 1 teaspoon unsalted butter*
*2 sweetbreads (approximately 1 1/2 pounds)*
*1 carrot, finely chopped*
*1 onion, finely chopped*
*1 shallot, finely chopped*
*1 thyme leaf or 1/4 teaspoon dried thyme*
*1 bay leaf*
*salt and pepper*
*1 tablespoon plus 1 teaspoon olive oil*
*6 cepes or any fresh mushrooms*
*1/2 cup port wine*
*1/2 cup chicken consomme*
*country bread, sliced*

1) Melt 1 tablespoon of the butter in a skillet and saute the sweetbreads over high heat for 5 minutes or until browned. Stir them constantly.

2) Mix the chopped onion, carrot, and shallot, and add them to the skillet. Season with the thyme, bay leaf, salt, and pepper. Cook this mixture over medium heat for 15 minutes.

3) Remove the sweetbreads from the skillet. Take out the thyme leaf (if used) and the bay leaf. Remove the skillet from the heat.

4) In another skillet, heat the olive oil and melt another tablespoon of the butter. Saute the mushrooms for 1 minute, then add the vegetables from the other pan. Remove the skillet from the heat.

5) Cut the sweetbreads into 1/2-inch cubes and mix them into

the vegetables in the skillet.

6) Preheat the oven to 375.

7) Rub the outside of the quails with the remaining 1 teaspoon of butter and one of oil. Divide the stuffing mixture in half and use one portion to stuff the four quails.

8) Roast the quails 8 to 10 minutes on each side, until they are brown. Skim the excess fat from the drippings and reserve.

9) Arrange the slices of country bread on a serving platter. Place the quails in the center of the platter.

10) Add the drippings, port wine, and consomme to the remaining half of the stuffing, and serve this as a sauce to accompany the quails.

## POMMES PAILLASON
### (Straw Potatoes)

*10 small potatoes*
*1 tablespoon olive oil*
*1 tablespoon unsalted butter*
*salt and pepper to taste*

1) Peel the potatoes and slice them into matchstick-size pieces, thinner than julienne strips, using a mandoline or a shredder.

2) Heat the oil and butter and saute the potatoes for 15 to 20 minutes, until they are crisp and golden brown.

## SALADE

1/2 cup olive oil
1 1/2 tablespoons white wine vinegar
1/4 teaspoon salt
1/4 teaspoon pepper
1/2 teaspoon chopped chives
1 head red-leaf lettuce

Shake the oil, vinegar, and seasonings in a tightly-covered jar. Refrigerate until ready to serve. Shake again before serving. Wash the lettuce, shake it dry, and tear it into bite-size pieces. Toss it with the dressing.

## FROMAGE
### (Cheese)

In the French culinary tradition cheese is always served after the salad and before the dessert. The Embassy chef recommends the following selections to complement this meal:

*Epoisse*
*Marroilles*
*Farmhouse Pyramid (Goat)*

*"Cheese compliments a good meal and supplements a bad one,, says Chef Layrle.*

## CHARLOTTE AUX FRAMBOISES
### (Vanilla Cream with Raspberry Sauce)

*3 gelatin sheets*
*warm water*
*2 cups whole milk*
*1 vanilla bean*
*1/2 cup plus 4 tablespoons sugar*
*5 egg yolks*
*1 cup heavy cream, whipped*
*1 box Biscuits a la Cuiller (tea biscuits available at most stores)*
*light sugar syrup (1 tablespoon sugar dissolved in 1/2 cup water)*
*1 teaspoon rum*
*1 pound fresh raspberries*
*juice of fresh lemon*

Special equipment: one standard 6-cup charlotte mold or other mold with straight sides

1) Soften the gelatin sheets in the warm water until soft and pliable.

2) Heat the milk with the vanilla bean to just below boiling point. Remove the vanilla bean.

3) Mix 1/2 cup of the sugar with the egg yolks in a saucepan. Gradually add the warmed milk. Cook gently over low heat, stirring constantly with a wooden spoon, until the mixture coats the spoon. Do not boil.

4) Add the softened gelatin sheets to the preparation. Put the pan in cold water until the vanilla cream begins to get firm, then fold in the whipped cream.

5) Add the rum to the sugar syrup, and then soften the Biscuits a la Cuiller in it. Line the charlotte mold with the moistened biscuits, making a design in the bottom and trimming where

necessary.

6) Pour the vanilla cream into the mold and refrigerate it.

7) To make the sauce, combine the raspberries, the remaining 4 tablespoons of sugar, and the lemon juice, and mix at medium speed until smooth.

8) To serve, remove the cream from the refrigerator and dip the mold in hot water for 30 seconds. Turn it upside down on a serving plate, then wait 15 minutes. Remove the pan.

9) Pour some of the raspberry sauce over the vanilla cream mold, reserving the rest to be passed to the guests at the table.

# THE EMBASSY OF THE FEDERAL REPUBLIC OF GERMANY

*Dinner for Six*

### LACHS TIMBALE MIT LANGUSTEN SAUCE
*(Salmon Timbale with Lobster Sauce)*

### SELLERIE SALAT MIT TRAUBEN UND NUESSEN
*(Celery Salad with Grapes and Nuts)*

### KALBSROLLE MIT PFIFFERLINGEN
*(Stuffed Veal with Pfifferlinge Mushrooms)*

### KARTOFFEL PUREE MIT ROSETTE
*(Duchess Potatoes)*

### SCHWARZWAELDER KIRSCH MOUSSE
*(Black Forest Chocolate Mousse)*

## WINES

SCHLOSS GROENESTEYN KIEDRICHER SANDGRUB 1983
SCHLIENGENER SONNENSTUECK SPAETBURGUNDER
SPATLESE 1983
HENKELL TROCKEN (SEKT)

The Embassy of the Federal Republic of Germany has the most avant-garde design of all the Washington, D.C. embassies. The chancery, built on a terraced hillside by the Berlin architect professor Egon Eiermann in 1954, is a monumental series of six glass balconies framed in light steel and Oregon pine. The building is an integral part of hilly terrain and comfortably accommodates a staff of one hundred seventy, all of whom have a view of the trees, the rocks, and the hillside. Architect Eiermann's governing architectural concept was philosophical: "May this house not only be an embassy, but have a mission as well."

On the same wooded parkland, the residence of H. E. Ambassador Gunther van Well and his beautiful American wife, Carolyn Bradley van Well, of Short Hills, New Jersey, contrasts with the modern windowed chancery. It is a handsome sprawling white country house with large windows overlooking gardens, and tall bushes surrounding a large patio, where they love to entertain.

The very large embassy parties of fifty or more are held in the six-tiered glass chancery, and the ambassador's intimate dinners are served in his residence.

The van Wells love politics, food, music, dancing, and entertaining. Their guests are famous German leaders of today: Chancellor Helmut Kohl and former Chancellors Helmut Schmidt and Willy Brandt, as well as members of the N.A.T.O countries, and United States government leaders, including President Reagan. Other celebrations recognize the achievements of leaders in the arts and government from the past and present: Henry Kissinger, Bruno Walter, and Erich Fromm to Richard Wagner, Bertolt Brecht, and Thomas Mann. Each is an occasion for a charming party serving fabulous German food.

The Germans love bread, beer, and *wurst*. The German Embassy's food, prepared by Chef Leonardo, an expert with unusually intricate meat dishes, features specialties, as well as fresh fruits, vegetables, mushrooms, cheese and special desserts. Chef Leonardo is an artist as well as a chef.

At the parties, German wines and beer are always served and the glasses are raised to the toast of Germany: "Zum Wohle" which translates, " To Your Health."

## LACHS TIMBALE MIT LANGUSTEN SAUCE
### (Salmon Timbale with Lobster Sauce)

*1 pound fresh salmon, cleaned, skinned, and boned*
*2 eggs plus one yolk, room temperature*
*2 1/2 cups heavy cream, room temperature*
*salt and pepper to taste*
*LOBSTER SAUCE (see following page)*

1) Preheat the oven to 375.

2) In a food processor, puree the salmon until smooth. Transfer to a bowl.

3) Beat the eggs, and stir in the cream. Pour this into the salmon puree little by little until the mixture is creamy and thick.

4) Add salt and pepper to taste and put the mixed ingredients into individual molds or a non-stick muffin pan. Bake in a *bain-marie* (water bath) for 45 minutes.

5) Serve the salmon timbale hot, pouring a little of the LOBSTER SAUCE over the individual portions. Pass the remaining sauce at the table.

## LOBSTER SAUCE

*2 pounds fresh, whole lobster*
*1 cup German Riesling (white) wine*
*3 cups fish stock, or bouillon cubes*
*BECHAMEL SAUCE (see following page)*
*1/8 teaspoon saffron powder*
*3 egg yolks, beaten*
*salt and pepper to taste*
*2 tablespoons fresh dill, finely chopped*

1) Cook the lobster(s) in the wine and fish stock. Bring the liquid to a boil, drop the lobster(s) in, let it return to the boil, and simmer for 20 minutes.

2) Remove the meat from the claws and tail and set aside. Reserve the broth.

3) Pound the remaining lobster shells (head, body, small legs) to release the juices. Return the pounded shells to the reserved broth and boil again for 5 minutes. Strain the broth and discard the lobster shells.

4) In a blender at high speed, blend the lobster meat with the reserved broth. Continue until the mixture liquifies to the consistency of whole milk. Thicken with BECHAMEL SAUCE, as needed.

5) Once the lobster mixture is thickened, add the saffron to taste, and then add the three beaten egg yolks and stir the sauce vigorously over low heat; do not allow it to boil or the sauce will curdle. Add salt, pepper, and dill.

### BECHAMEL SAUCE

*1/4 pound sweet butter*
*1/2 tablespoon cornstarch*
*l/2 cup whole, fresh milk*


1)   Melt the butter in a small pan and stir in the cornstarch. Stir until dissolved.

2)   Lower heat to very low and add the milk slowly, in a steady stream, stirring well.

## SELLERIE SALAT MIT TRAUBEN UND NUESSEN
### (Celery Salad with Grapes and Nuts)

*2 pounds fresh celery root, julienned*
*4 stalks celery, cut at an angle into 1-inch pieces*
*1 large apple, cored and cut into 1/4-inch cubes (do not peel)*
*6 ounces fresh or canned pineapple, cut into small, fork-size*
*    chunks*
*6 ounces black walnut meats*
*3/4 cup seedless grapes, halved*
*1/2 cup currants, preferably fresh*
*1 1/2 cups mayonnaise*

*FOR THE DRESSING:*

*1/4 cup granulated white sugar*
*1/4 cup red wine vinegar*
*1/4 cup olive oil*
*salt and pepper to taste*

1) Prepare the salad dressing; mix all the ingredients in a bowl and set aside.

2) Mix the fruits and vegetables in a bowl and toss thoroughly. Add the dressing. Chill from 2 to 4 hours before serving.

3) Just before serving, add the mayonnaise. Serve while cool.

## KALBSROLLE MIT PFIFFERLINGEN
### (Stuffed Veal with Pfifferlinge Mushrooms)

1 pound veal kidneys (3 small or 2 large)
3 pounds round roast of veal
1/4 teaspoon marjoram
1 teaspoon chopped basil
4 thick strips bacon
salt and pepper to taste
1 1/4 pound pfifferlinge mushrooms
4 tablespoons (1/2 stick) sweet butter
1 bunch parsley, chopped
PFIFFERLINGE SAUCE (see following page)

1)  Preheat the oven to 350.

2)  Remove the fat and the white tube from the kidneys and soak in cold water for 20 minutes.

3)  Broil the kidneys 8 to l0 minutes.

4)  Using a long, slim knife, punch a hole all the way through the veal roast lengthwise. Stuff the broiled kidneys into the hole, cutting them to size if necessary.  Make sure they are evenly distributed.

5)  Sprinkle the roast with the marjoram, basil, and salt and pepper to taste.  Wrap the veal with the four strips of bacon.

6)  Cook until tender, about 1 1/2 hours.

7)  When done, set aside but keep warm.  Reserve the drippings.

8)  Saute the pfifferlinge in the butter.  Reserve 4 tablespoons for the PFIFFERLINGE SAUCE and add the parsley to the rest.

Season with salt and pepper to taste.

9) To serve, slice the veal into 1/4-inch slices, spoon the PFIFFERLINGE SAUCE over them, and pass the sauteed pfifferlinge in a separate dish.

## PFIFFERLINGE SAUCE

*1/4 pound unsalted butter*
*2 tablespoons all-purpose white flour*
*1 teaspoon shallots, chopped very fine*
*2 8-ounce cans beef broth*
*1/2 cup heavy cream*
*Reserved veal drippings*
*Reserved pfifferlinge mushrooms*

1) In a medium-size saucepan melt the butter. Stir in the flour, and cook over medium heat until the mixture is brown.

2) In a separate pan, saute the shallots, then mix them with the flour and butter.

3) Over low heat, pour in the beef broth, stirring well. Add the cream slowly, and then the reserved veal roast drippings. Mix well.

4) Next add the pffifferlinge. Keep warm.

### KARTOFFEL PUREE MIT ROSETTE
#### (Duchess Potatoes)

*6 large Idaho potatoes*
*1/4 pound (1 stick) unsalted butter, at room temperature*
*1 teaspoon ground nutmeg*
*salt and pepper to taste*
*3 egg yolks, beaten*

1) Bake the potatoes at 450 for 45 minutes or until tender. Scoop out the insides; discard skins. Turn oven up to broil.

2) Using an electric mixer, beat the potatoes. Add the butter, nutmeg, and salt and pepper while the mixer is running.

3) Put the mixture in a pastry bag; pipe six large rosettes. Brush with beaten egg yolk.

4) Broil for about 1 minute, or until brown. Keep warm until ready to serve.

## SCHWARZWAELDER KIRSCH MOUSSE
### (Black Forest Chocolate Mousse)

2 pounds canned cherries, pitted
1/2 cup Kirsch
10 1/2 ounces semisweet chocolate
1/2 cup half and half
2 envelopes unflavored gelatin
1/2 cup granulated white sugar
4 egg yolks, beaten
1 3/4 cups heavy whipping cream
8 ounces Marzipan

FOR THE SAUCE:

2 packages frozen raspberries
1/4 cup Kirsch

1)  Soak the cherries in the Kirsch overnight.

2)  In a double boiler, melt 10 ounces of the chocolate in the half and half.

3)  Dissolve the gelatin in 1/4 cup cold water.

4)  When the chocolate is melted, add the sugar, egg yolks, and gelatin; stir constantly until creamy.  Do not boil. Put aside to cool at room temperature, but do not allow to set.

5)  Whip 1 cup of the heavy cream and fold it into the chocolate mixture. Keep this slightly warm.

6) Line the sides of a springform pan (6 inches in diameter and 3 1/2 to 4 inches deep) with Marzipan. (Use a rolling pin to make a strip as long as the circumference of the pan and as wide as the depth.) This Marzipan shell, when baked, will hold the filling in. Note: do not put any marzipan on the bottom of the pan.

7) Pour half of the chocolate mixture into the baking form; chill until firm. Evenly distribute the cherries over the chocolate, reserving some for garnish. Pour remaining chocolate into the shell.

8) Refrigerate for 6 hours, or, preferably, overnight.

9) Remove the baking form from the refrigerator and put the mousse in the center of a 14- to 16-inch circular platter.

10) Whip 1/4 cup cream and spread it on the top of the mousse. Decorate with the reserved cherries and chocolate curls shaved from the reserved 1/2 ounce of chocolate.

11) Make the sauce: Put the thawed raspberries into a blender with the Kirsch and liquify. Strain and pour around the mousse on the platter.

12) Whip the remaining 1/2 cup cream and put it in a pastry bag. Using the small tip, make four concentric circles of whipped cream on top of the sauce, around the mousse. Leave a distance between the rings so the red syrup shows.

13) With a sharp knife or a toothpick, draw lines in the syrup and whipped cream, starting at the edge of the mousse and moving outward toward the edge of the plate. The spokes should be 1 to 1 1/2 inches apart at the outer edge. Serve cold.

# EMBASSY OF THE UNITED KINGDOM OF GREAT BRITAIN AND NORTHERN IRELAND

*Dinner for Eight*

SMOKED SALMON WITH SALMON MOUSSE

FILET OF SOLE WITH SAUCE PORTO AND SAUCE CHAMPAGNE

ROLLED ROAST OF VEAL WITH MUSHROOM DUXELLE, SAUCE MADEIRA

OVEN-ROASTED POTATOES
BABY CARROTS
BABY PEAS

TERRINE DE FROMAGE BLANC
*(Cream Cheese Mousse)*

DEMITASSE

WINES
White Wine with the Salmon
White Wine with the Filet of Sole
Both Red and White offered with the Veal
Champagne served with the Cream Cheese Mousse

# UNITED KINGDOM OF GREAT BRITAIN AND NORTHERN IRELAND

The Embassy of Great Britain and Northern Ireland, with its Great Houses and staff of 500, dominates Washington D.C.'s Embassy Row. Negotiating the coded elevators and doors from the main building to Ambassador Sir Oliver Wright's office is like taking a tour of the maze at Hampton Court. There are red brick chateaux, gardens, a huge chancery, the elegant residence of the Wrights, a large glassed-in reception hall, and individual apartments for the staff. It is all very glamorous and reminiscent of the country palaces of Great Britain.

Standing in front of the iron gates and elaborate gardens, facing the avenue, is a 15-foot bronze statue of Sir Winston Churchill, right hand raised high in the V-for-victory salute, left hand at his side holding the inevitable cigar. Early every morning a member of the embassy staff places fresh flowers or colored leaves through the fingers of the left hand.

Behind the official buildings is a large garden, where each June the Queen's birthday is celebrated with a strawberries-and-cream festival, complete with champagne, strolling musicians, and proud, haughty peacocks.

As you enter the ambassador's residence, where most of the formal entertaining takes place, you are greeted by 8-foot, gold-framed paintings of former dashing British kings and queens, some on horseback, some posed on the throne. The most beautiful is an exquisite painting of Queen Elizabeth wearing a white sequinned gown and the royal crown.

The drawing rooms and dining rooms are palatial, decorated with Persian rugs, paintings, and crystal chandeliers. They are formal, but comfortable and bright. In contrast to this opulent elegance, the kitchen is all business. As befits a room where dinners for thirty are prepared several times a week, this is a hotel-type stainless steel working area, with multiple ovens, ranges, sinks, refrigerators, and working tables.

All meals are prepared and supervised by Chef Yasao Kawano, an expert chef trained in Japan, London, and Lyon, France. He has been with the British Embassy for over three years, and has presided over the dinners served to Queen Elizabeth and Prince Philip, Prince Charles and Lady Diana, Princess Margaret, Margaret Thatcher, and many notables of the United States government.

Chef Kawano, wielding his pots and pans, whirls through the steel kitchen with the flair and grace of a Baryshnikov. He prepared the following menu for us, watching every detail, and then hovered over us as we sampled each course. We assured him it was delicious, a meal "fit for a King."

The visit of Prince Charles and Lady Diana was one of the highlights of Ambassador and Lady Wright's years in Washington D.C.:

"I don't think any of us expected people would sleep in the open outside the Washington Cathedral or J.C. Penney's just to catch a glimpse of them in the morning," remarked the ambassador.

Ambassador and Lady Wright recently returned to England. They are missed. The ambassador had this final quote on leaving:

"If it be now, 'tis not to come;
If it be not to come, it will be now;
If it be not now, yet it will come...
The readiness is all."

Hamlet, Act 5

A farewell champagne toast to Sir Oliver and Lady Wright:
"Cheers...and Good Luck."

## UNITED KINGDOM OF GREAT BRITAIN AND NORTHERN IRELAND

### SMOKED SALMON WITH SALMON MOUSSE

*2 pounds smoked salmon, half sliced paper-thin and*
  *half sliced at regular thickness*
*1/2 pint heavy cream*
*juice of 1/2 lemon*
*1/2 medium cucumber*
*1 small carrot*
*1 bunch watercress (for garnish)*

1) Select 16 pieces of the thinly-sliced salmon, each about 4 inches square. Place each piece flat on a piece of wax paper.

2) Put the remainder of the salmon, the cream, and the lemon juice into a food processor. Whip until smooth and easily spreadable.

3) Spread the mousse evenly onto the slices of salmon.

4) Seed the half cucumber and clean the carrot. Cut each into strips about the thickness of the lead in a pencil. Place in separate bowls of cold water if necessary to maintain crispness.

5) Place four or five pieces of cucumber and four or five pieces of carrot crosswise in the center of each salmon slice. Roll the salmon around the sticks, like a jelly roll. Once the roll is begun, it should be easy to continue it by lifting the wax paper.

6) Put two of the rolls on each of eight plates and decorate them with a sprinkling of carrot and cucumber strips. Lay a sprig of watercress between the rolls on each plate.

7) Serve slightly chilled.

## FILET OF SOLE WITH SAUCE PORTO AND SAUCE CHAMPAGNE

*16 filets of fresh sole, approximately 3 by 2 1/2 inches*
*1 pound of fresh sole, skinned and cleaned*
*2 egg whites*
*1/4 teaspoon salt*
*1/2 pint heavy cream*
*4 cups fish stock (bouillon cubes may be used)*
*SAUCE PORTO (see below)*
*SAUCE CHAMPAGNE (see below)*

1) Preheat the oven to 350.  Lay the filets out flat on a work surface.

2) Put the pound of sole, the egg whites, and the salt into a food processor; whip until smooth.  Transfer the mixture to a deep bowl and gradually fold in the cream.

3) Place 2 tablespoons of the sole mousse on the widest half of each sole filet, and fold the other end over it, tucking in the edges so that none of the filling spills out.

4) Reserve 1 teaspoon of the bouillon; put the rest into a baking dish (approximately 16 by 8 inches).  Arrange the filets evenly in the dish, cover with a piece of wax paper, and tuck the paper in around the edges.  Bake for 4 minutes.

5) Remove the filets from the baking dish and place in two rows of eight on a serving platter.  Cover one row with SAUCE PORTO and the other with SAUCE CHAMPAGNE.

### SAUCE PORTO

*3/4 cup port wine (Tawny or Sandemans)*
*1 cup heavy cream*
*1/2 teaspoon fish stock or bouillon*

Simmer the port over low heat until it is reduced to 1/2 cup, about 3 minutes. Add the cream a little at a time, stirring constantly. Add the stock or bouillon and boil for another 3 minutes. Keep warm until ready to serve.

### SAUCE CHAMPAGNE

*3/4 cup champagne*
*1 cup heavy cream*
*1/2 teaspoon fish stock or bouillon*

Simmer the champagne over low heat until it is reduced to 1/2 cup, about 3 minutes. Add the cream a little at a time, stirring constantly. Add the fish stock or bouillon and boil for another 3 minutes. Keep warm until ready to serve.

## ROLLED ROAST OF VEAL WITH MUSHROOM DUXELLE, SAUCE MADEIRA

1 5-pound boneless loin of veal, about 14 inches long and 3
  inches in  diameter
salt and pepper
1/4 pound butter
1 onion, finely chopped
1 pound mushrooms, finely chopped
1/2 cup heavy cream
HOLLANDAISE  SAUCE (see following page)
watercress (for garnish)
SAUCE  MADEIRA (see following page)

1) Lightly salt and pepper the veal.  Roast in a 350-degree oven for 20 minutes.  Cool and slice into 16 pieces about 1/2-inch thick.

2) Prepare the mushroom duxelle: saute the mushrooms and onion (you may chop these in a food processor) in the butter for 5 minutes.

3) Spread about 1 tablespoon of the duxelle on each of eight slices of the veal.  This should use about half the duxelle.  Place the other eight slices of veal on top of the duxelle to make sandwiches.  Put the sandwiches into a loaf pan, about 14  by 4 and 3 inches deep.

4) Preheat the oven to 350.

5) Heat the heavy cream just to the scalding point.  Add the remaining duxelle; stir for 3 minutes.  Remove from heat and add the HOLLANDAISE SAUCE.  Spread this mixture over the veal loaf, and bake for 5 minutes.

6) To serve, separate the sandwiches and serve one to each guest.  Decorate with watercress.  Pass the SAUCE MADEIRA separately.

# UNITED KINGDOM OF GREAT BRITAIN AND NORTHERN IRELAND

### HOLLANDAISE SAUCE

*1/4 cup water*
*3 egg yolks*
*1/2 cup melted butter*

Heat the water in the top of a double boiler. Add the egg yolks and beat constantly over low heat for 4 minutes. Add the butter very slowly, turn off the heat and continue to beat until the sauce is thickened to the consistency of lightly whipped cream.

### SAUCE MADEIRA

*3/4 cup Madeira*
*1 cup beef stock or bouillon*

Simmer the Madeira for 5 minutes or until reduced slightly. Add the beef stock or bouillon and cook an additional 3 minutes over low heat. Serve separately, in a gravy boat or sauciery.

Decorate with watercress.

Each guest is served one veal sandwich with mushrooms duxelle as the filling and HOLLANDAISE SAUCE with mushrooms and cream over the top as the garnish. SAUCE MADEIRA is served separartely.

### OVEN-ROASTED POTATOES

*1/4 tablespoon butter*
*8 small potatoes (about 2 inches in diameter), peeled*
*salt to taste*
*2 tablespoons fresh parsley, chopped*

Use the butter to grease a pan large enough for the potatoes to remain separate. Sprinkle the potatoes with salt and roast for 30 minutes in a 350-degree oven. Garnish with the parsley before serving.

### BABY CARROTS

*16 small carrots*
*1 tablespoon sugar*
*1/2 tablespoon salt*
*2 tablespoons butter*

Scrape the carrots and place in a pan with water to cover, the sugar, the salt, and the butter. Boil for 10 minutes or until tender.

Scrape the carrots and place in a pan with water to cover, the sugar, the salt, and the butter. Boil for 10 minutes or until tender.

## BABY PEAS

2 pounds fresh young peas, in pods
salt to taste
1/4 tablespoon butter

Shell the peas and place them in a pan with water to cover and salt to taste. Bring to a boil and cook for 5 minutes. Drain and saute over medium heat in the butter for 1 minute.

## TERRINE DE FROMAGE BLANC
### (Cream Cheese Mousse)

1/2 pound cream cheese
3/4 cup sugar
1/2 cup sour cream
2 egg yolks
1/2 teaspoon vanilla
juice of one lemon
rind of one lemon, finely grated
2 packages unflavored gelatin, dissolved in 1/2 cup boiling water
1 1/2 cups heavy whipping cream
raspberries, strawberries, or slivered almonds for garnish

2) Whip the cream. Fold 1 cup of it into the cream cheese mixture and reserve the rest for topping.

3) Pour the mixture into a mold (8 by 4 by 4-inch) and chill until set, approximately 30 to 45 minutes.

4) Unmold the terrine (dipping it into hot water for 30 seconds will facilitate removal) onto a serving dish. Cover it with the remaining whipped cream as if icing a cake. Decorate with berries or almonds and cut into eight slices.

## THE EMBASSY OF GREECE

*Dinner for Ten*

### TARAMOSALATA
*(Fish Roe Dip)*

### OUZO

### BAKED FISH A LA SPETSIOTA

### BOUTI ARNIOU
*(Leg of Lamb with Grape Leaves)*

### PATATES STO FOURNO
*(Baked Potatoes, Greek Style)*

### ELLINIKI SALATA
*(Greek Salad)*

### GALAKTOBOUREKO
*(Cream Pie)*

### GREEK COFFEE

### WINES
*Nemea Hercules*
*Chateau Claus*
*Mauvodaphne*

As guests arrive for a gala evening at the Embassy of Greece on Massachusetts Avenue, they are personally greeted by Ambassador and Madame George Papoulias, standing atop a red-carpeted stairway leading to the grand ballroom. The ambassador and his wife, both tall, blond, and gracious, have a warm handclasp or a kiss on the cheek for everyone.

Beyond them is the dazzling ballroom, with its Doric columns, Louis XVI chairs and tables, colorful paintings, and crystal chandeliers. At its center is a fully-equipped stage, and at each end are gold-and-white doors leading to reception rooms. The room can accommodate several hundred people for drinks and hors d'oeuvres. Tables are decorated with fruits, flowers, and candles, and spread with marvelous appetizers: grape leaves stuffed with rice and nuts; hot cheese pastries; bite-size lamb shish kebabs with peppers, onions, and olives; a great plate of salmon; and platters of select cheeses and rich pastries.

The more formal, seated dinners, where Ambassador and Madame Papoulias are host to twenty-five to thirty guests, are held in the large dark-oak panelled room to the left of the ballroom. The room is rich and inviting with its elaborately-carved fireplace and warm, indirect lighting.

Ambassador Papoulias and Madame have supplied us with a sample menu served at one of their formal dinners. This meal, like so many at the embassy, is the culmination of subtle refinements to Greek cuisine that have been made not just over the years, but over the centuries. There is a saying: "When Greek meets Greek, they start a restaurant." And why not? The tradition of Greek cooking began a thousand years before the birth of Christ, when the Greeks were already making twenty different kinds of bread. Menus enjoyed by Plato and Homer nine hundred years ago would meet the approval of Frixos Economou, the chef of the Greek Embassy today.

Greek cooking is rich and Greek hospitality is warm; eating and drinking are highlights of life, to be shared by friend and stranger alike. The country's cuisine varies markedly from region to region, an evolution due in part to the influences of invaders–Bulgars, Goths, Visigoths, Romans, Slavs, and Avars–and in part to Greece's one-time status as a world power, dominating Asia, Cyprus, France, and Spain.

Invading Huns, in 500 A.D., appalled the Corinthian Greeks by using knives at the table, and by eating butter. The Greeks used only olive oil in cooking—butter was a skin conditioner. And as for table manners, meat was cut before being brought to the table, and fowl was eaten by hand. Slices of bread were used as napkins and then given to the dogs.

It was the Turks who introduced the Greeks to the glories of garlic, and Turks returning home from Greek-occupied lands brought with them such foods as cheese, figs, olives, and honey.

Now, Ambassador and Madame Papoulias share their hospitality with you and invite you to sample a truly magnificent cuisine, prepared by Chef Frixos Economou. Served with wines such as Nemea Hercules, Chateau Claus, and Mavrodaphne, it is, literally and figuratively, a meal "fit for a king." As the Greeks would say, "Stin Iya Sas!". . ."To Your Health!"

## TARAMOSALATA
(Fish Roe Dip)


*1/3 of 1 8-ounce jar tarama (carp roe)*
*1 small onion, finely grated*
*1 1/2 cups olive oil*
*4 1/2 slices white bread, trimmed*
*juice of 2 lemons*
*unsalted crackers or toast*


1) In a blender or food processor, combine the tarama, the onion, and 1/4 cup of the olive oil.  Process until the mixture is a smooth paste.

2)  Moisten the bread and then squeeze out excess water.

3) Continue processing the tarama mixture, adding alternately small amounts of the bread, the remaining 1 1/4 cups of olive oil, and the lemon juice.  Process until the taramosalata is creamy-orange.

4) Serve this as a dip with unsalted crackers or as a spread on toast.

Serve with OUZO:  the famous Greek liquor served with the TARAMOSALATA.  Put the OUZO in a small glass.  Add ice and water.  It will turn milky, taste like anisette, and is a strong, delicious, pre-dinner cocktail.

## BAKED FISH A LA SPETSIOTA

10 filets (about 1/2 pound each) of rockfish, red snapper,
  or grouper
salt and pepper to taste
juice of 1 lemon
1/2 cup dry white wine
1 cup water
3 pounds onions, sliced
1/3 cup olive oil
2 bay leaves
10 ounces tomato paste
6 cloves garlic, minced
1/2 bunch parsley, chopped
1/2 pound fresh ripe tomatoes, sliced

1) The night before serving, rinse the filets and drain them. Place them in a 12 by 14-inch roasting pan, leaving some space between each filet. Add the salt and pepper, lemon juice, and wine. Cover the pan with plastic wrap and refrigerate it overnight.

2) To make the sauce, boil the water, onions, oil, and bay leaves over low heat for 1/2 hour. Add the tomato paste and garlic. Continue cooking for 1 more hour, or until the sauce becomes thick and creamy. Stir about every 15 minutes.

3) Preheat the oven to 400.

4) Remove the sauce from the heat, take out the bay leaves, and puree it in a food processor or a blender. Add the parsley.

5) Pour the sauce over the fish and place the sliced tomatoes on top. Bake for 15 minutes. The fish can be served hot or cold.

## BOUTI ARNIOU
(Leg of Lamb with Grape Leaves)

*1 16-ounce jar grape leaves*
*1 5-pound boneless leg of lamb (the bone may be reserved; see*
*    step 7)*
*1/4 pound Gruyere, cubed*
*1/2 bunch fresh mint, chopped*
*4 cloves garlic, mashed*
*3 tablespoons grated Parmesan*
*1 tablespoon oil*
*2 carrots, coarsely chopped*
*1 celery stalk, coarsely chopped*
*1/2 cup dry white wine*
*juice of 1 fresh lemon*
*1 tablespoon cornstarch, dissoved in 1/4 cup cold water*

1) Preheat oven to 450.

2) Blanch the grape leaves in boiling water. Drain them and remove any stiff stalks.

3) Spread the grape leaves on a table, overlapping each other, until a rectangle large enough to wrap the leg of lamb is formed.

4) Put the leg of lamb on the grape leaves. Spread it with a mixture of the Gruyere, mint, garlic, and Parmesan. Fold the meat over the filling, and then fold the grape leaves tightly around the lamb.

5) Cut two pieces of heavy-duty aluminum foil large enough to wrap around the meat. Place one sheet of foil under the meat and brush the inside of the top sheet with the oil. Seal the foil tightly to secure the juices.

6) Tie the roast with kitchen string and place it in a roasting pan with about a cup of water.

7) Arrange the carrots, celery, and lamb bone, if available, in the roasting pan.

8) Bake the lamb for 1 hour, then reduce the heat to 400, turn the roast, and continue cooking for 2 more hours.

9) To prepare the gravy, open the foil and pour the juices into a saucepan with the carrots and celery. Bring this to a boil, then strain it, return it to the pan, and add the wine and lemon juice. Simmer it for a few minutes, then thicken it with the cornstarch.

10) Slice the meat into 1/2-inch slices, and serve it with the gravy and with PATATES STO FOURNO (following recipe).

### PATATES STO FOURNO
(Baked Potatoes, Greek Style)

*3 pounds medium-size potatoes, peeled*
*juice of 1 fresh lemon*
*1 teaspoon oregano*
*4 ounces butter, melted*
*4 cups beef or chicken stock*
*salt and pepper to taste*

1)  Preheat the oven to 450.

2) Wash the potatoes and cut each one lengthwise into four thick slices.   Place them in a roasting pan with all the other ingredients, and roast for about 1 1/2 hours, basting occasionally. Add stock or water if the pan becomes dry.  Remove the potatoes from the oven when they are slightly brown.

### ELLINIKI SALATA
(Greek Salad)

*2 heads romaine, torn into bite-size pieces*
*6 medium tomatoes, cut into wedges*
*1 cucumber, thinly sliced*
*1 green pepper, coarsely chopped*
*1 bunch scallions, chopped*
*1 cup black Greek olives*
*1/4 pound feta cheese, broken into chunks*
*vinegar*
*olive oil*
*oregano to taste*
*salt and pepper*

1) In a salad bowl, mix the lettuce, tomatoes, cucumber, green pepper, scallions, and olives.

2) Sprinkle the feta cheese chunks overall.

3) Make the dressing with one part vinegar to three parts olive oil; add the seasonings to taste. Dress the salad just before serving.

## GALAKTOBOUREKO
### (Cream Pie)

*5 1/2 cups milk*
*peel of 1/2 lemon*
*9 eggs*
*1 1/4 cups sugar*
*3 ounces rice flour*
*2 ounces fine semolina*
*1 cup heavy cream*
*1 teaspoon vanilla*
*1 pound frozen phyllo dough*
*12 ounces unsalted butter, melted*
*SYRUP (see following page)*

1) In a large saucepan, boil the milk with the lemon peel, then remove the peel.

2) Beat the eggs with the sugar until they are a pale lemony color. Add the rice flour and the semolina.

3) Over low heat, pour the egg mixture gradually into the hot milk, stirring constantly. Heat this combination for 3 or 4 minutes, or until it reaches the consistency of heavy cream.

4) Remove the pan from the heat and stir in the cream and vanilla.

5) Preheat the oven to 350.

6) Grease a 12 by 14 by 2-inch baking pan. Place a sheet of phyllo dough into the pan, with the edges hanging over the sides. Brush it with butter. Repeat this procedure until 2/3 of the phyllo is used.

7) Pour the cream filling onto the phyllo. Fold the edges of the sheets over the filling. Cover this with the remaining sheets, brushing each one with butter. With a sharp knife, make lengthwise cuts through the top layer.

8) Bake the pie for 90 minutes. Remove it from the oven and immediately pour cold SYRUP (see below) over it. Let it cool and cut it into squares or diamond-shaped pieces.

### SYRUP

*2 1/4 cups sugar*
*9 ounces water*
*1 cinnamon stick*
*2 cloves*
*juice and peel of 1/2 lemon*

Combine all the ingredients in a saucepan and boil them for 10 minutes. Let the syrup cool and remove the lemon peel and cinnamon stick.

# THE EMBASSY OF THE
# HUNGARIAN PEOPLE'S REPUBLIC

*Dinner for Six*

## CONSOMME

## GULYAS
*(Goulash)*

## KOLOZSVARI TOLTOTT KAPOSZTA
*(Stuffed Cabbage)*

## CSIRKE PAPRIKAS GALUSKAVAL
*(Chicken Paprika with Dumplings)*

## MARHA PORKOLT
*(Hungarian Beef Stew)*

## CREPES PALACSINTA
*(Simple Crepes)*

## BEVERAGES

## PALINKA
*(Hungarian aperitif)*

## PUSZTA COCKTAIL
*(Tokay wine, palinka, and bitters)*

## EGRI BIKAVER
*(Red Wine)*

## BADACSONYI KEKNYELU
*(White Wine)*

## TOKAY ASZU
*(Dessert wine)*

The Embassy of the Hungarian People's Republic is a complex of white brick and stone buildings overlooking a park. A stream, a tiny waterfall, and an old mill are complemented in summer by brilliant flowers. Strangely, all this quiet beauty is situated only a few blocks from the bustling, roaring traffic of Washington's Connecticut Avenue.

The compound includes three large buildings: the official residence of Ambassador (Dr.) Vencel Hazi and his wife, Judit; a large chancery (office building), graced by an enormous mural of Budapest on one wall of the reception room; and a third building houses staff members.

The Hungarian approach to entertaining is warm and hospitable. The embassy staff told us: "Hungarian food is a personal, homey cuisine. The delicate tastes must express one's personality...the best in oneself...we prepare each dish with loving care. Each represents your feelings toward your guests."

The chief cook of the Hungarian Embassy is Maria Kejla, who arrived in this country three years ago. She is assisted in preparing for big parties by the wives of the diplomatic staff. Each wife has a special recipe, taught to her by her mother, and each is a specialist in one traditional Hungarian dish. There are no arguments nor recipe-stealing in the huge kitchen.

Hungary's unique cuisine developed out of nomadic Asiatic traditions. In the first century, Hungary was occupied by the Romans, who planted grapes, grains, and fruit trees in the fertile basin. Next the Magyars, the nomadic horsemen from the Ural Mountains, settled around the Danube River and introduced meat stews, milk, and cream, which in due course evolved into today's famous Hungarian *gulyas* (goulash).

In the sixteenth century the Austrians, Russians, and Turks influenced Hungarian cooking. It was during the Turkish invasion that paprika, that sweet spice indispensable to Hungarian cuisine, was introduced. Szeged, the paprika capital, boasts acres of sweet red peppers, which are dried and ground into paprika.

The dishes offered here, through the hospitality of the

embassy and Ambassador Vencel Hazi and his wife, Madame Judit Hazi, represent some of the great Hungarian specialties. Among these is Hungary's national dish, *guylas*, which means shepherd's stew. Traditionally, the sherpherds cooked this dish over an outdoor fire in a large kettle called *bogracs*. They boiled chunks of beef with vegetables, and seasoned it with their highly-prized sweet paprika.

Another of the more famous dishes in the Hungarian cuisine is *csirke paprikas* (chicken paprika). It is prepared with the common Hungarian combination of sour cream and sweet paprika.

The paprika-flavored stew made from pork, veal, or beef is uniquely Hungarian in the way the flavor is derived by "scorching" the meat, a process that gave the dish its name, *porkolt*.

The menu here provided by Ambassador and Madame Hazi is specially selected to offer a variety of "favorite recipes" that may be combined in various ways to make a gracious dinner for the most sophisticated palates.

The meal is complemented by traditional Hungarian spirits, and many toasts "To Your Health!"

## CONSOMME

*2 pounds beef bones*
*1 ounce kohlrabi*
*1 green pepper*
*2 ounces green cabbage*
*5 ounces carrots*
*2 ounces celery*
*2 ounces parsnips*
*1 ounce onions*
*1 ounce fresh mushrooms*
*1 large clove garlic, crushed*
*1 ounce tomato puree*
*1 teaspoon salt*
*5 black peppercorns*
*1 cup narrow egg noodles*

1) Wash the beef bones, place them in 4 pints of water, and bring to a boil. Reduce the heat and simmer for 10 minutes. Skim off the fat.

2) Add the washed vegetables, the garlic, the tomato puree, the salt, and the pepper. Simmer for 3 hours. Strain and set vegetables aside.

3) Remove 4 cups of the broth and place in a separate saucepan. Add the egg noodles and cook for 9 minutes.

4) While the noodles are cooking, chop the vegetables finely.

5) Return the noodles and vegetables to the broth in the original pot. Bring to a boil, remove from heat and serve.

## GULYAS
### (Goulash)

*2 pounds chuck roast or stew meat, cut into 3/4-inch cubes*
*2 tablespoons lard*
*2 large onions, coarsely chopped*
*2-3 tablespoons sweet Hungarian paprika*
*3 medium potatoes, diced*
*2 medium tomatoes, finely chopped*

1) Pat each piece of meat dry. In a large saucepan saute the meat in the lard until brown. Push the meat to one side.

2) In the empty area of the saucepan, saute the onions until tender and light pink. Use more lard if necessary.

3) Stir in the paprika and mix thoroughly; cook for about 1 minute. Add water to cover. Cook slowly for 1 hour. As this goulash recipe calls for no flour, it will thicken only with *slow* cooking.

4) Add the potatoes and tomatoes and continue cooking for another 30 minutes or until potatoes and meat are tender.

5) Serve in soup bowls with chunks of French bread.

## KOLOZSVARI TOLTOTT KAPOSZTA
### (Stuffed Cabbage)

*1/4 pound rice*
*6 large or 12 small cabbage leaves*
*2 pounds sauerkraut*
*1/4 pound onion, finely chopped*
*1 medium clove garlic, crushed*
*3 ounces lard*
*1 pound ground pork*
*1 egg*
*1/8 teaspoon ground pepper*
*1/8 teaspoon marjoram*
*1/2 teaspoon sweet Hungarian paprika*
*salt to taste*
*7 ounces spicy smoked sausage, thinly sliced*
*1/2 pint sour cream*
*2 ounces all-purpose flour*

1)  Preheat oven to 350.

2)  Cook the rice and allow to cool.

3) With a sharp knife remove the thick rib from the center of each cabbage leaf to make it more pliable.

4) Taste the sauerkraut. If it's too sour or salty, rinse it.  Set aside.

5) Saute the onion and garlic in 1 ounce of the lard.  Divide in half and set aside.

6) Place the ground pork in a bowl and add the rice, half the onion-garlic mixture, the egg, pepper, marjoram, and half the paprika. Mix well. This will be the stuffing mixture.

7) Place 1/6 or 1/12 of the stuffing mixture in the middle of each cabbage leaf; fold the edges over the stuffing and roll tightly.

8) Grease a 10 by 10 by 2-inch pan with the remaining lard. Evenly distribute the sauerkraut in the pan, and spread the remaining onion-garlic mixture, salt, and paprika across the top.

9) Arrange the stuffed cabbage leaves on the sauerkraut and cover them with the sausage slices. Cover the pan and bake 1 3/4 hours.

10) When cooked, remove the cabbage rolls and sausage and thicken the sauerkraut as follows: Reserve 2 tablespoons of the sour cream; mix the rest with the flour and stir into the kraut. Cook on top of the stove for about 10 minutes.

11) Transfer the kraut to a deep dish and place the cabbage rolls and sausage on top. Garnish with the rest of the sour cream and serve hot.

## CSIRKE PAPRIKAS GALUSKAVAL
### (Chicken Paprika with Dumplings)

*2 frying chickens, about 3 pounds each, cut up*
*4 tablespoons lard*
*2 medium onions, chopped*
*2 garlic cloves, crushed*
*3 tablespoons Hungarian paprika*
*1 1/2 cups chicken broth*
*salt and pepper to taste*
*2 tablespoons flour*
*2 cups sour cream*
*DUMPLINGS (see following page)*

1) Wash chicken pieces and pat dry. Heat the lard in an 8-inch skillet, and fry chicken on both sides until golden brown, about 15 minutes. Remove from pan and keep warm.

2) Remove all but one tablespoon of the drippings, and add the onions and garlic. Saute until tender and translucent. Add the paprika and cook for one minute; stir. Mix in the chicken broth and bring to a boil. Season with salt and pepper.

3) Return the chicken pieces to the skillet, cover, and cook slowly until tender, about 45 minutes. Add more broth during cooking if needed. Remove to a warm platter.

4) Combine the flour and the sour cream and add to the skillet. Cook slowly, stirring until thickened and smooth. Return the chicken to the sauce.

5) Garnish with DUMPLINGS and serve hot.

### DUMPLINGS

*2 teaspoons salt*
*3 eggs, well beaten*
*1/2 cup water*
*2 cups all-purpose flour*

1) Heat 8 cups of water and 1 teaspoon of the salt to boiling in a Dutch oven. Mix the eggs, the 1/2 cup water, the flour, and the rest of the salt in a large bowl and knead into dough.

2) Drop the dough, a teaspoonful at a time, into the boiling water.

3) Cook at a boil, uncovered, stirring occasionally, for 10 minutes. Drain. The dumplings should be chewy.

## MARHA PORKOLT
### (Hungarian Beef Stew)

*2 pounds lean beef, cut into 1-inch cubes*
*3 tablespoons lard*
*1/2 pound onions, peeled and sliced*
*1 tablespoon Hungarian red paprika*
*1 medium-size tomato, cut into 1/2-inch cubes*
*1 green pepper, cleaned and cut into 3/4-inch squares*
*1/3 pint sour cream*

1) Rinse the meat and pat it dry with a paper towel.

2) Melt the lard in a thick-bottomed pot 4 inches deep and 10 inches in diameter. Saute the onions until tender.

3) Take the pan off the heat and cool slightly; add the paprika. Return to the burner over high heat. Add the beef and "scorch" it (brown it very thoroughly). Stir constantly. When the meat is dark brown, add the tomato, green pepper, and salt to taste.

4) Reduce the heat and allow to simmer, covered, about 45 minutes. The meat should cook in liquid, so add a little water occasionally if necessary. When the meat is tender, the onions will be soft enough to form a thick sauce when stirred.

5) Just before serving, add the sour cream and bring the porkolt to a quick boil. Serve hot with boiled potatoes.

Note: PORKOLT can be made with pork or veal. Whatever is used, it is the scorching that gives the dish its unique flavor. Characteristically, PORKOLT has an abundance of onions and rich, thick sauce.

## CREPES PALACSINTA
### (Simple Crepes)

1/2 pint cold milk
2 eggs
9 ounces semolina flour
7 ounces soda water
1/2 ounce sugar
1/4 pound lard
Powdered sugar
Apricot jam or lemon juice

1) Mix the milk and the eggs using a wire whisk. Add the flour slowly while continuing to mix. When completely free of lumps, add soda until the dough is the consistency of cream. Add the sugar. The batter should be very thin.

2) Melt the lard in a small saucepan. Heat a clean crepe pan. Add less than a teaspoon of the melted lard to the crepe pan, and swirl it around until the bottom of the pan is covered. Drain the excess batter back into the saucepan.

3) Pour about 3 1/2 ounces of the dough onto the crepe pan, and swirl it around. Use a high heat and shake the pan continuously. The dough should not stick. Cook on one side for 5 or more seconds, then turn and cook the other side. If the crepe does not stay together, add an egg or a little flour.

4) After all the crepes are cooked, sprinkle them with powdered sugar and serve with Hungarian apricot jam. Or, sprinkle them with lemon juice, roll them up, and dust with powdered sugar.

THE EMBASSY OF INDIA

*Dinner for Four*

KASHMIRI ROGAN JOSH
*(Kashmiri Lamb)*

KHEEMA MATTAR
*(Minced Lamb with Green Peas)*

KOFTA
*(Lamb or Beef Croquettes)*

MACHLI CURRY
*(Fish Curry)*

ALU SABZI
*(Spiced Fried Potatoes)*

MURGH TIKHA LAHORI
*(Barbequed Chicken)*

GAJAR HALVA
*(Carrot Dessert with Almonds)*

A. M. Rosenthal, the executive editor of *The New York Times*, reminisced recently: "When I was young, and writing from India, I embraced the gift of each day. Each day was filled with sound and movement, with thought and action, with a delighted awareness of the present, hope for the future and the sense of the rolling of history.... When I think of my four reporting years there, I see myself surrounded by people, motion, color, joy and sorrow; and kindly friends; by heat, rain, the scent of dung and of the marigold, snow on the mountain, muck in the village, anger, laughter, elegance and decay...." He continued: "India is the sense of color and dash in the dress of every Rajasthani woman brick-carrier. It is the music everywhere. It is the dozen different countries and races and religions roiling in the one India. It is the warmth of the people, so kind, so loving, the adventure in travel, and the still-existing greatest adventure–the Indian adventure in freedom."

Indian cuisine is also an adventure in color, in taste, and in exotica. With several thousand years of history, a terrain that ranges from pine to palm tress, from rolling oceans to perpetually snow-capped mountains, this cuisine is as diverse as the face of India, and even more dazzling.

Here art and life are one. Conversation, costume, food, and drink are arts taken as seriously as painting and sculpture; there is none of the detachment regarded as good form in the West. The colors, textures, and smells of mounds of spices—tumeric, ginger, chiles, garlic–are an artistic expression to a citizen of India.

His Excellency, Indian Ambassador Pretap Kishan Kaul and Madame Kaul receive their guests at the ambassador's sumptuous residence located on a hill overlooking Washington, D.C.'s wooded Rock Creek Park. The mansion is elegantly furnished with Indian art of gold and marble. Vivid carpets and colorful decor represent India's many moods: from the serenity of the Taj Mahal at sundown to the bustling streets of New Delhi.

One of India's most eloquent representatives in the United

States is public relations executive Janki Ganju. Born in Kashmir, he has been India's secret weapon in Washington during the presidencies of Eisenhower, Kennedy, Johnson, Nixon, Ford, Carter, and Reagan. From 1966 to 1982, he arranged the visits of Prime Minister Indira Gandhi. And in 1985, he did the same for Prime Minister Rajiv Gandhi. He has advised on many banquets and receptions for heads of state, sometimes cooking the dishes himself.

Indians serve several main dishes at their important dinners. Mr. Ganju describes the menu that follows, as a composite Indian feast, representing all parts of India, highlighting regional dishes.

An Indian dinner is served on a huge oblong table, covered with a bright saffron or red or purple cloth and a centerpiece of fresh fruits, often decorated with flowers. All of the dishes are placed on the table and the guests help themselves. As soon as one serving plate is empty, an exotic Indian woman in a brilliant sari whisks it away and returns with a full platter.

American, French and German wines are served with dinner, although Ganju sometimes serves beer to cool the hot and spicy dishes. It is, as Ganju says,"a feast for the eyes, the tongue, and the stomach."

# *INDIA*

### KASHMIRI ROGAN JOSH
### (Kashmiri Lamb)

*2 pounds lamb, preferably front leg, cubed*
*2 1/2 cups water*
*8 tablespoons vegetable oil*
*salt to taste*
*4 whole cloves*
*pinch of asafoetida*
*1 tablespoon powdered ginger*
*1 tablespoon  powdered red chili*
*1 2-inch stick cinnamon*
*pinch of saffron*
*6 tablespoons yogurt, beaten lightly*

1) Put 2 cups of the water in an 8-inch, heavy saucepan.  Add all the rest of the ingredients except the saffron and yogurt.

2) Cook, uncovered, over high heat until all the water evaporates–about 10 minutes.  Add the remaining 1/2 cup of water, cover, and simmer for 1 1/2 hours or until the meat is tender.

3) Add the saffron and yogurt and continue cooking over low heat until the gravy is reduced and thickened.

## KHEEMA MATTAR
(Minced Lamb with Green Peas)

*1 pound ground meat (lamb or beef)*
*2 tablespoons vegetable oil*
*4 whole cloves*
*1 large black cardamom pod, slightly crushed*
*2 green chilis*
*1 large onion, finely chopped*
*2 tomatoes, chopped*
*2 cloves garlic, minced*
*1 tablespoon turmeric*
*1/2 tablespoon powdered ginger*
*salt to taste*
*2 sticks cinnamon*
*1/2 pound green peas*
*coriander leaves, chopped, for garnish*

1) In a large skillet, heat the oil and saute the cloves, cardamom pod, and chilis. Add the chopped onion and cook until it browns.

2) Stir in the tomatoes, meat, garlic, turmeric, ginger, salt, and cinnamon sticks. Cover and cook until the meat is almost tender–about half an hour. Add the peas and cook a few minutes longer.

3) Before serving, remove the cardamom pod and the cinnamon sticks. Garnish with the chopped coriander leaves.

## KOFTA
### (Lamb or Beef Croquettes)

*1 pound ground lamb or beef*
*8 tablespoons vegetable oil*
*1 cup yogurt*
*4 whole cloves*
*pinch of asafoetida*
*salt to taste*
*1 egg*
*1 tablespoon chili powder*
*1 tablespoon powdered ginger*
*1 tablespoon coriander*
*1 tablespoon cumin seeds*


1) Shape the ground meat into four koftas–sausage-shaped rolls about 3 or 4 inches long and 1 to 1 1/2 inches thick.

2) In a heavy skillet, place the oil, half the cup of yogurt, the cloves, and the asafoetida.  When it simmers, put in the koftas and continue cooking, shaking the skillet from time to time to prevent them from sticking to the bottom.

3) Add all the other ingredients, including the other half-cup yogurt.  Cover and cook over medium heat for about 15 minutes, or until the gravy is reduced and the koftas are browned.

4) Serve on a hot platter and garnish with small vegetables, such as peas, carrots and chilis.

### MACHLI CURRY
(Fish Curry)

2-pound trout, flounder or rock fish
8 or more tablespoons vegetable oil
pinch of asafoetida
salt to taste
1 tablespoon tamarind paste
2 green chilis, chopped
1 tablespoon powdered ginger
1 tablespoon turmeric
1 cup water
parsley, for garnish

1) Clean the fish, remove the head and tail, and de-bone. Cut the flesh into 2-inch pieces, and deep-fry them in 6 or more tablespoons of the oil (enough to cover) until golden brown.

2) In a separate pan, heat 2 tablespoons of oil and saute the asafoetida, salt, tamarind paste, chilis, and ginger briefly.

3) Add the turmeric, the fish and the water. Cook for three minutes. Remove to a serving platter, garnish with parsley, and serve with lemon butter.

## ALU SABZI
### (Spiced Fried Potatoes)

*6 medium-size potatoes*
*4 tablespoons cooking oil*
*1/2 teaspoon black mustard seeds*
*1/2 teaspoon whole cumin seeds*
*1 onion, coarsely chopped*
*1 green chili, minced fine*
*3 garlic cloves, minced fine*
*2 tablespoons freshly-grated ginger*
*salt to taste*
*1 teaspoon turmeric*
*1/2 teaspoon cayenne*
*2 large ripe tomatoes, chopped*
*2 tablespoons fresh coriander, chopped*
*Squeeze of fresh lemon juice*

1) Boil the potatoes for about 20 minutes (they should still be firm).  Peel them and cut them into 1/2 inch cubes.

2) Heat the oil in a large skillet and fry the mustard and cumin seeds, covering the skillet for protection from popping seeds.

3)  Add the onions, chili, garlic, and ginger.  Fry for 2 minutes.

4) Add the potatoes, salt, turmeric, and cayenne.  Fry, stirring once or twice, for 2 or 3 minutes.  Stir in the tomatoes and cook for about 10 minutes more, stirring occasionally.  Put in the coriander and lemon juice, and serve.

## MURGH TIKHA LAHORI
### (Barbequed Chicken)

1 1/2-pound chicken
1 tablespoon plain yogurt
juice of 1 lemon
2 cloves garlic, crushed
1/2 teaspoon freshly-grated ginger
salt and pepper to taste
pinch of ground cardamom
pinch of cinnamon
pinch of ground cloves
1/4 teaspoon red chili powder
1 teaspoon paprika
2 tablespoons corn oil
2 tablespoons butter, melted

1) One day before serving, skin the chicken and cut it into four pieces. Slash the pieces all over so that the marinade will permeate well.

2) In a deep bowl, prepare the marinade by combining all the remaining ingredients except the melted butter. Place the chicken pieces in the marinade, turning and spooning the sauce over the meat to coat well. Cover and refrigerate for 24 hours, turning every few hours so the sauce covers the meat evenly.

3) When ready to cook, brush the chicken pieces with the butter and cook over a charcoal fire or in the broiler. Baste occasionally with the marinade and turn often. The chicken should cook until nicely browned. Serve very hot with buttered rice.

## GAJAR HALVA
### (Carrot Dessert with Almonds)

*1 pound carrots, finely grated*
*2 cups half and half*
*1/2 cup light brown sugar*
*1/2 cup golden raisins*
*1/4 cup unsalted butter*
*1/2 teaspoon ground cardamom*
*1/4 teaspoon salt or to taste*
*1/4 cup chopped almonds or pistachios*

1) Heat the carrots and the half and half to boiling in a 2 quart saucepan. Reduce heat, cover, and simmer, stirring frequently, until the liquid is absorbed. This will take about 1 hour.

2) Stir in the brown sugar, raisins, butter, cardamom and salt. Simmer over low heat, stirring constantly, until the sugar is dissolved–about 15 minutes. Garnish with the almonds or pistachios and serve.

THE EMBASSY OF THE
REPUBLIC OF INDONESIA

*Dinner for Eight*

SOTO AYAM
*(Chicken Ginger Soup)*

NASI GURIH
*(Rice Cooked in Coconut Milk)*

SATAY AYAM/DAGING
*(Chicken and Meat Barbeque with Peanut Sauce)*

MEDAN'S SALAD
*(Pineapple and Vegetable Salad with Peanut Dressing)*

TAHU KETOPRAK
*(Beancurd Salad with Peanut Sauce)*

IKAN ACAR KUNING
*(Fish with Spicy Pickled Sauce)*

PERKEDEL JAGUNG
*(Corn Fritters)*

# REPUBLIC OF INDONESIA

Indonesia, an archipelago of 13,677 islands, is the world's most populous Moslem country, and ranks fifth among all nations in population. Java, Sumatra, Sulawesi, Kalimantan, and New Guinea (now called Irian Jaya) are just a few of the fabulously romantic islands to be found there.

Marco Polo was the first European to visit the archipelago, in 1292. Then came the Portuguese, looking for spices, then the Dutch; then, during World War II, the Japanese. After the Japanese surrender in August 1945, the Indonesian people proclaimed their independence through their national leaders, President Sukarno and Vice President Mohammed Hatta, and a new day of freedom was born for Indonesia.

Ambassador Soesilo Soedarrman and his wife, Widaning Sri, have recently arrived in Washington, D.C. They preside over an early nineteenth century mansion on Massachusetts Avenue's Embassy Row. It is rich with brilliant Indonesian paintings, books, and exquisitely carved sculptures, and musical instruments from Java and Bali. The Soedarrmans enjoy organizing bazaars, international discussion groups, and performances of traditional Javanese and Balinese dances.

Indonesia's great culinary tradition is *Rijsttafel*, a meal that is a culmination of more than 1,000 years of the cultural, political and economic history of the 3,000 Spice Islands. The word means simply "rice table," but the meal includes the foods and spices of the Asians, the Europeans, and the Americans. The tradition grew during the years of colonial opulence. Guests were seated around long tables laden with fine imported linens, china, crystal, and silver; they were served soups, curries, seafood, poultry, lamb, beef. Today, however, the emphasis is on "nouvelle Indonesian cuisine" with a sophisticated balance of lighter but still full-flavored sauces, from spicy sweet soy to fiery chili.

To prepare the recipes for this book, ten Indonesian women from the embassy were gracious enough to cook, sample and serve each dish. It took six weeks for them to arrive at the perfect combination of tastes and flavorings—the perfect blend of sweet, sour, spicy and smooth recipes. Each recipe is a statement of the individual cook's personality.

All the ingredients for these recipes may be obtained at one's local supermarket, an Asian market, or a specialty food store. A good light beer or tea (hot or iced) are the best beverages with spicy Indonesian food. Wine, cool and light, may be served before the meal as an introduction to the Indonesian dishes. Fresh fruit is an appropriate dessert.

### SOTO AYAM
(Chicken Ginger Soup)

*1 whole chicken, cut up*
*1 tablespoon vinegar*
*salt to taste*
*6 candlenuts or unsalted Macadamia nuts*
*1 teaspoon turmeric*
*3 cloves garlic*
*1 2-inch piece fresh ginger, peeled*
*1 teaspoon pepper*
*2 medium-sized onions, quartered*
*1 2-inch piece fresh lemon grass (available in international food*
  *markets) or the juice of 2 lemons*
*CONDIMENTS (see following page)*
*SAMBAL  KEMIRI (Hot Chili Sauce; see following page)*

1) Put the chicken pieces in a pot with water to cover, the vinegar, and the salt.  Bring to a boil.

2) Put the nuts, turmeric, garlic, ginger, pepper, and onions into a food processor or blender and grind to a fine paste.  Add salt as needed.

3) Add the spice paste and the lemon grass or lemon juice to the boiling soup and cook over medium heat until the meat separates from the bones–about 1 hour.

4) Remove the chicken pieces; scrape the chicken from the bones with a fork.  Discard the bones and return the chicken to the pot.  Remove the lemon grass if used.  The soup may be served as is, or made into a clear broth by straining through cheesecloth, chilling, and removing the fat layer.

5) To serve, put the soup in a large tureen in the center of the table and surround it with the various condiments, each in a 4-inch rice bowl. The guests may serve themselves. The rice or vermicelli and the bean sprouts should be put into the bowls before the soup; the rest of the condiments, including the chili sauce, are stirred into the soup afterward.

### CONDIMENTS

*2 cups fresh bean sprouts, blanched*
*2 cups vermicelli, broken into small pieces and soaked in hot*
  *water*
*5 stalks celery, finely sliced*
*1 bunch onion greens, finely sliced*
*1 cup scallion greens, sliced paper-thin and fried in hot oil*
  *or 1 cup dried onion flakes fried in hot oil*
*2 cups potatoes, sliced paper-thin and fried in hot oil*
  *or 2 cups unsalted potato chips*

Serve with 2 cups cooked white rice.

### SAMBAL KEMIRI
(Hot Chili Sauce)

*8 fresh red chilis*
*8 candlenuts or unsalted Macadamia nuts*
*salt to taste*
*juice of 1 lemon*

Put all the ingredients into a blender or food processor and grind to a smooth paste. If necessary, add chicken stock to moisten.

# REPUBLIC OF INDONESIA

## NASI GURIH
### (Rice Cooked in Coconut Milk)

*4 cups long-grain rice*
*7 cups coconut milk*
*2 sticks lemon grass, or juice of 2 lemons*
*5 bay leaves, slightly crumbled*
*pinch of salt*

1) Wash the rice three times, drain, and put it in a rice cooker with the coconut milk, lemon grass, bay leaves and salt. Bring the rice to a quick boil, remove the bay leaves and lemon grass, and cook until the rice cooker turns itself off. Wait for 5 or 10 minutes before serving. This is richer and more aromatic than plain white rice.

2) If you do not have a rice cooker, wash the rice the same way and combine all the ingredients in a heavy dutch oven with a tight-fitting cover. Bring to a boil, stir quickly, remove the bay leaves and the lemon grass, and cover the pot. Turn the heat to low and simmer undisturbed for 20 minutes. Remove from the heat without removing the cover, and allow to stand for 15 minutes. Fluff and serve.

### SATAY AYAM/DAGING
(Chicken and Meat Barbeque with Peanut Sauce)

*6 boneless chicken breasts, cut into 3/4-inch cubes*
*1 pound rump side lamb, cut into 3/4-inch cubes*
*3 tablespoons soy sauce*
*1 teaspoon garlic, minced*
*2 tablespoons vegetable oil*
*1 teaspoon lime juice*
*PEANUT SAUCE (see below)*

1) Mix the soy sauce, garlic, vegetable oil, and lime juice. Marinate the meat in this mixture for at least 1 hour.

2) Put five to six cubes of the marinated meat on each of 25 bamboo skewers, and grill them over charcoal, turning them occasionally until the meat is done. If not serving them immediately, keep them warm in the oven.

3) Serve the meat hot, with the SAUCE (see below) in a small dish for dipping or spooning over it.

### PEANUT SAUCE

*1 cup roasted peanuts, chopped*
*1/4 cup shallots, chopped*
*1 teaspoon garlic powder*
*1 tablespoon red chili peppers, chopped*
*1/2 cup sweet soy sauce*
*pinch of sugar*
*salt to taste*

Mix all the ingredients together, and serve with the barbequed meat.

## MEDAN'S SALAD
### (Pineapple and Vegetable Salad with Peanut Dressing)

*1 ripe pineapple, cored, peeled, and diced*
*1 1/2 cups cucumber, peeled and thinly sliced*
*4 cups lettuce, sliced*
*4 cups large potatoes, very thinly sliced*
*3 cups tomatoes, thinly sliced*

### PEANUT DRESSING

*2 tablespoons paprika powder*
*2 cups water*
*1 pound peanut butter*
*1/3 cup sugar*
*pinch of salt*
*4 tablespoons vinegar*

1) Place the pineapple and the vegetables on a large serving plate.

2) To make the dressing, stir the paprika powder into the water and boil down for about 10 minutes, until half a cup remains. Chill.

3) Combine the peanut butter, sugar, and salt. Pour this over the paprika liquid, place in a blender, and process until smooth. Add the vinegar.

4) Pour the dressing over the fruit and vegetable platter.

### TAHU KETOPRAK
(Beancurd Salad with Peanut Sauce)

*4 large pieces tofu, cut in 3/4-inch cubes*
*2 or more tablespoons vegetable oil*
*2 cups bean sprouts*
*1/2 cup celery, chopped*
*1/2 cup spring onions or scallions, chopped*
*1/4 cup shallots, sliced and fried*
*1/2 cup shrimp chips (available in Asian food markets)*
*PEANUT SAUCE (see below)*

1) Fry the tofu cubes in the oil for 2 to 3 minutes. Place them on a serving plate.

2) Soak the bean sprouts in hot water for 5 minutes. Drain them and add them to the tofu.

3) Sprinkle the chopped celery and fried shallots on top and arrange the shrimp chips around the outside of the plate.

4) Pour the PEANUT SAUCE over the plate just before serving.

#### PEANUT SAUCE

*1 cup roasted peanuts or 1/4 cup peanut butter*
*1 large red chili*
*2 cloves garlic*
*1 tablespoon brown sugar*
*1/4 cup sweet soy sauce*
*1/4 cup lukewarm water*
*1 tablespoon vinegar*
*salt to taste*

Place the ingredients in a food processor or blender and grind until smooth.

## IKAN ACAR KUNING
### (Fish with Spicy Pickled Sauce)

1 2-pound red snapper, rock fish, or flounder
vegetable oil for deep frying

### SPICY PICKLED SAUCE

1/2 cup onions, chopped
3 cloves of garlic
4 candlenuts or unsalted Macadamia nuts
1/2 teaspoon turmeric
2 tablespoons peanut oil
2 cups water
1/3 cup white vinegar
1 tablespoon sugar, or to taste
1/2 stalk lemon grass
1/2 inch fresh ginger
pinch of salt
1 carrot, scraped and shredded
2 fresh red chilis, sliced
1/2 cup green bell pepper slices
1/4 pound small fresh mushrooms

1) Clean and scale the fish, leaving the skin intact. Wash the inside of the fish; dry thoroughly. Heat 2 inches of oil in a wok or a 12-inch frying pan and fry the fish over medium heat, turning once or twice, about 7 minutes on a side, until golden brown and slightly crisp. Remove the fish from the oil and keep it warm.

2)  To make the sauce, make a paste of the onions, garlic, candle-nuts, and turmeric.  This can be done with a mortar and pestle or in a blender.  Heat the oil in the wok or skillet and saute the seasoning paste for about 3 minutes, stirring frequently.  Put in the water, vinegar, sugar, lemon grass, and ginger and bring to a boil.  Season with salt.  Turn the heat down and simmer until thick—about 10 minutes.  Remove from the heat and stir in the raw vegetables.

3)  Transfer the fish to a serving plate and pour the sauce over it.

### PERKEDEL JAGUNG
### (Corn Fritters)

*6 ears fresh young corn*
*1 egg*
*1 teaspoon salt*
*1 medium-size onion, chopped*
*2 cloves garlic, minced*
*1 teaspoon coriander*
*1/2 teaspoon cumin powder*
*1/2 cup self-rising flour*
*vegetable oil for deep frying*
*1 cup confectioners sugar*

1) Scrape the corn kernels from the cob and chop them. Put them in a blender and add the egg, the salt, the onion, the garlic, the coriander, the cumin powder, and last, the flour. Blend at medium speed until thoroughly mixed.

2) Heat the oil in a deep 12-inch skillet. Form the dough into fritters with a tablespoon and deep fry them for 10 minutes in the hot oil until light brown.

3) Drain the fritters.

4) Dust lightly with confectioners sugar.

THE EMBASSY OF ISRAEL

*Dinner for Six*

BABA GHANOUJ
*(Eggplant with Tahini)*

CREAMED HERRING

BOUREKAS
*(A Cheese, Spinach, and Egg Pie, –A Knish)*

CARROT SALAD

CHOLENT
*(Sabbath Stew)*

HONEY CAKE


BEVERAGES

SANGRIA
SABRA
TURKISH COFFEE

# ISRAEL

Ambassador Meir Rosenne of Israel smiled broadly when asked to describe a typical formal dinner at the Israeli Embassy. He explained that Israeli food is an international composite of all the cultures that have made up his country, dating all the way back to Biblical times.

Restaurants in Tel Aviv or Jerusalem often feature French, British, Arab, or German delicacies. Since the Israeli people have come from all over the world, the origin of the foods they prepare extends to Russia, Greece, Turkey, and even to the Orient. Menus are a symphony of delights–corned beef from the British Jews who immigrated to Israel after the Independence of 1948, grape leaves stuffed with rice and lamb *(warak enab)*, Turkish coffee, Russian winter borscht, Greek moussaka, Oriental spices, and always the oranges, tomatoes, olives, and grapes from Jaffa.

Ambassador and Madame Vera Rosenne are pleased to provide several recipes from which a variety of formal and informal dinners can be conceived. They are taken from the menus served not only at the embassy, but also in Tel Aviv, Jerusalem, Bethlehem, and from regions around the Dead Sea and the Judean Desert.

Of course, there is that extra something that comes from being served a dinner in the new and exquisite Israeli Embassy on International Drive in Northwest Washington, D.C. It has the grace and gentleness of typical Jerusalem architecture. It blends in perfectly with the park it overlooks.

The following menu and recipes will bring you the special flavors of Israel, the country with one hundred and one tastes. They are all "strictly kosher"–meat and milk products have not been mixed. They reflect the many varied cultures of Israel.

From Jerusalem to Washington, D.C. the well-loved Israeli toast is "L'Chayim!" . . . "To Life!"

### BABA GHANOUJ
(Eggplant with Tahini)

1 large eggplant
1 medium onion
1/2 bunch parsley
1/2 cup tahini (sesame seed paste)
2 tablespoons lemon juice, or to taste
2 cloves garlic, crushed
2 teaspoons cool water
1 teaspoon salt
pinch cayenne pepper
1 bunch parsley for garnish

1) Roast the eggplant directly over a gas burner until the skin chars and the inside becomes soft. Turn it frequently. This should take about 30 minutes. Or, bake it in a 450-degree oven until it is charred, about 30 minutes.

2) Let the eggplant cool slightly and cut it in half lengthwise. Scoop out the pulp–using a wooden spoon will preserve the flavor. Then chop the pulp fine in a ceramic or wooden bowl.

3) Grate the onion on the largest holes of a grater. Squeeze the juice out of it and discard. Chop the parsley very fine and then add the parsley and the squeezed onion to the eggplant. Mix well.

4) Blend the tahini thoroughly with the lemon juice and garlic. Stir in the water gradually until the mixture becomes white in color. Add this to the eggplant mixture, then add the salt and the cayenne pepper. Mix well. Serve with pita bread.

<br />

## *ISRAEL*

### CREAMED HERRING

10 *small herring*
1 *cup heavy cream*
2 *tablespoons sugar*
2 *tablespoons wine vinegar*
1 *medium onion, thinly sliced*

1)  Clean and filet the herring and cut each into five pieces.

2)  Whip the cream with the sugar; fold in the vinegar.

3)  Layer the filets and the onion slices in one or two 1-quart jars and pour the cream mixture over the layers.  Cover and let set overnight.

### BOUREKAS
(Cheese, Spinach, and Egg Pie)

1/2 *pound margarine*
3 *cups self-rising flour*
1 *teaspoon salt*
1/2 *cup feta cheese*
1 *cup spinach, chopped and cooked*
4 *egg yolks*
1/4 *cup roasted sesame seeds*

1)  Preheat the oven to 350.

<br />

<br />

<br />

132

2) To make the dough, melt the margarine. Mix the flour with the salt and stir them into the margarine. Add enough warm water to make the dough stick together, then roll it out to the thickness of a pie crust. Cut out six circles of dough 3 inches in diameter–the size of a coffee cup.

3) To make the stuffing, mix the feta, the spinach, and three of the egg yolks. Place 1 teaspoon of this mixture in the center of each circle of dough. Fold the dough over to form a semicircle.

4) Beat the last egg yolk and brush each boureka with it. Sprinkle them with the sesame seeds.

5) Place the bourekas on a greased cookie sheet and bake until golden brown, about 30 minutes.

## CARROT SALAD

*4 large carrots*
*1/2 cup raisins*
*1/4 cup fresh orange juice*
*1/2 teaspoon sugar*

1) Peel and grate the carrots.

2) Mix the grated carrots with the raisins, orange juice, and sugar. (Less or more sugar may be used, according to taste.)

3) Let the salad stand for 1 hour while preparing the rest of the meal.

## CHOLENT
### (Sabbath Stew)

2 cups dried lima beans
1 3-pound brisket of beef
3 medium-size onions, diced
3 tablespoons oil
2 teaspoons salt
1/4 teaspoon pepper
1/4 teaspoon powdered ginger
1 cup pearl barley
2 tablespoons all-purpose flour
2 teaspoons paprika

1) Soak the beans overnight in water to cover. Drain.

2) Using a heavy saucepan or a Dutch oven, brown the meat and the onions in the vegetable oil over high heat. When browned, reduce the heat to medium.

3) Sprinkle the meat with the salt, pepper and ginger. Add the beans and the barley, and sprinkle with the flour and paprika.

4) Add boiling water to a level of 1-inch over the stew ingredients. Cover tightly.

5) Cholent was traditionally baked for 24 hours in a 250-degree oven; for quicker cooking, bake at 350 for 4 to 5 hours. When done, slice the meat and serve with the barley and the beans.

Note: CHOLENT was an answer to the ancient problem of how to have nourishing, hot food on the Sabbath without violating Jewish traditional laws about lighting a fire on that special day. Since food could be prepared in advance and kept in a warm oven lighted before the Sabbath, CHOLENT was created. The process of long, slow cooking was developed, thus enhancing the flavor. This ancient dish is served only on weekends. It is a thick, heavy, and filling food—a "tiring" food—because after eating, one requires rest.

## HONEY CAKE

*3 1/2 cups all-purpose flour (sift before measuring)*
*1/4 teaspoon salt*
*1 1/2 teaspoons baking powder*
*1 teaspoon baking soda*
*1/2 teaspoon cinnamon*
*1/4 teaspoon nutmeg*
*1/8 teaspoon powdered cloves*
*1/2 teaspoon ground ginger*
*4 eggs, beaten lightly*
*3/4 cup sugar*
*4 tablespoons salad oil*
*2 cups dark honey*
*1/2 cup brewed coffee*
*1 1/2 cups walnuts or almonds, coarsely chopped*

1) Preheat the oven to 325.

2) Sift the flour, salt, baking powder, baking soda, cinnamon, nutmeg, cloves and ginger together. (Spices may be increased according to taste.)

2) While beating the eggs, gradually add the sugar. Beat until thick and light in color, then beat in the oil, honey and coffee. Stir in the flour mixture and the nuts.

3) Grease an 11 by 16 by 4-inch baking pan and line it with aluminum foil. Or use two 9-inch loaf pans, greased and lined.

4) Pour the batter into the pan or pans and bake for 1 1/4 hours (large pan) or 50 minutes (small pans). When the cake is browned on top, test with a cake tester or a straw, which should come out clean.

5) Cool the cake on a rack before removing it from the pan.

Note: Honey Cake is the traditional cake of the "Land of Milk and Honey." While delicious any time, Honey Cake is a must for the Jewish New Year, Rosh Hashanah, because it symbolizes in its sweetness the wishes for a good year ahead.

## BEVERAGES

Israelis are not in the habit of drinking alcoholic beverages. However, here are some party beverages served on special occasions.

### SANGRIA

*3 3/4 cups red dry wine*
*2/3 cup sugar*
*1 can peaches or apricots with syrup*
*2 cups bitter lemon or 7-Up*
*juice of half a lemon and 2 oranges*

Combine all ingredients in a large pitcher. Mix well and refridgerate 6 to 8 hours before serving.

## ISRAEL

### SABRA

SABRA is the name of a famous Israeli liqueur, exported abroad. Sabra is the nickname of Israeli native-born youths, who are compared to the thorny but sweet inside fruit of the cactus plant. SABRA is usually served chilled. It can be made into a cocktail by adding 2 teaspoons fresh lemon juice and 2 teaspoons lemon syrup into a chilled glass. When drinking a SABRA toast, it is appropriate to raise the glass and exclaim "Le Hayim" . . . "To Life."

### TURKISH COFFEE

TURKISH COFFEE is best prepared in the traditional *feenjan*, which can be purchased in any Eastern specialty store or department store. It is wide at the bottom, narrowing toward the top and has a long handle.

*1 tablespoon finely ground Turkish coffee*
*1 teaspoon sugar, depending on taste*
*cardamon pods, according to taste*
*boiling water*

Place coffee and sugar in a saucepan. Mix well. Add 1 serving cup boiling water. Bring coffee to the boil. When foam begins to rise, remove coffee from the heat until it settles. Repeat the process. Pour into a demitasse cup, spooning in some of the foam. Do not stir. Serve immediately. Multiply this recipe by whatever number is required for more than one cup.

THE EMBASSY ITALY

*Luncheon for Eight*

CONCHIGLIE CON SALSA DI ARAGOSTA
*(Pasta with Lobster Sauce)*

ARROSTO DI VITELLO RIPIENO
*(Milk-Fed Veal Roast)*

LEGUMI VARI
*(Mixed Vegetables)*

SORBETTO DI FRUTTA
*(Sorbet with Fresh Fruit)*

VINI
*(Wine)*

GAVI DI GAVI
BRUNELLO DI MONTALCINO (1975)
CHAMPAGNE GILARDINO BRUT

# ITALY

The beauty, vitality, and pleasure of Italian life is reflected by the loving way in which food is prepared. Italy is a country of sensuality; a country where music, art, love, and entertaining dominate everyday living. In Italy it is normal to have impassioned discussions about what coffee bar has the best hot pastries in the morning, or which restaurant has the finest artichokes, and where one might find the most unique *antipasto* and *primi piatti* (first courses) at dinner.

The Cultural Attache of the Italian Embassy in Washington, Piergiuseppe Bezzetri, a spare, aristocratic gentleman, was eloquent when he described his country's cuisine: "Exploring Italian cooking is a rich culture in itself...a symptom, a passport, a label, a melody of different cultures."

In 1875, Italy was divided into many states, each with a different cultural background. In the north, where the Dolomites are snow-capped all year, the cuisine is influenced by neighboring Austria and France, and there is an emphasis on cream in the sauces. In the Piedmont section, a specialty is Bechemel sauce, also rich with cream and butter. It is a well-known fact that when Catherine de Medici married the King of France, she was shocked by the lack of imagination in the cooking at the French Court, and made a return trip to Florence to collect some recipes for import to Paris.

Southern Italian cooking is influenced by the Arab occupation of the eighteenth century, and by a climate where olives, tomatoes, fruits, and nuts abound. The favorite dishes in this part of Italy are marinated fish with pine nuts and sweet peppers, and *Pasta a Fagioli*, a bean-and-pasta soup with plum tomatoes, basil, bacon, and chili peppers. These dishes are now also served frequently in the north, in Venice and Florence.

In Milan, the gastronomic capital of central Italy, *Risotto a la Milanese* (rice prepared with saffron and beef marrow) is the most famous dish since Medieval times. It is enjoyed now by all the operatic stars of La Scala.

Although the Italians still eat formal meals that include soup, a meat or fish course, salad, and dessert, their menus are changing.  They tend to eat more grains in the form of pasta and rice, as well as more fresh vegetables and fruits.

His Excellency Ambassador Rinaldo Petrignani and Madame Petrignani came to Washington, D.C. last year from Rome after serving in Brussels.  They brought their chef, Marc Colle from Belgium, with them to their residence, which is called Firenze House.  Chef Colle presides over three kitchens, equipped with a myriad of shiny pots and pans.  He also oversees an enormous vegetable, herb, and flower garden.

Firenze House is famous in Washington for its Italian splendor—enormous floor-to-ceiling windows, original Italian paintings, and dark oak paneling, brightened by vases of pink and white flowers.  It is the scene of frequent lunches and dinners for anywhere from twenty-four to several hundred guests.

President Ronald Reagan was entertained at a luncheon at Firenze House on October 12, 1983.  Chef Colle was kind enough to provide the menu from that occasion for inclusion here.

Chef di Cuisine, Marc Colle, has worked at his art for more than 20 years.  In addition to the President of the United States, he has served the vice president, White House officials, members of Congress, and foreign heads of state.  He is the proud holder of no less than thirteen medals and awards honoring his "novelle and classique cuisine."

Dining at the Italian Embassy is a classic drama of marvelous food.  The appetizer is Act I; the entree is the elegant climax; and the dessert, the denouement.  With fine Italian Champagne, Chef Colle and the embassy toast you:  "Aguri"..."Best Wishes."

## CONCHIGLIE CON SALSA DI ARAGOSTA
### (Pasta with Lobster Sauce)

1 *pound medium-size seashell pasta (about 10 cups)*
*l/2 teaspoon salt*
*1 tablespoon butter*
*LOBSTER SAUCE (see following page)*

l)  Bring 4 to 6 quarts of water to a boil.  Add the salt and the pasta, and cook for 9 minutes.  Drain.

2)  Mix the pasta with the butter and put into a warmed serving dish.  Top with the LOBSTER SAUCE.  Garnish with the lobster meat reserved after making the SAUCE.

### LOBSTER SAUCE

*1 1/2 pounds fresh lobster, cut up*
*pinch of salt*
*freshly ground pepper*
*2 sprigs parsley*
*1 sprig thyme*
*1/2 bay leaf*
*14 tablespoons butter (1 3/4 sticks)*
*2 tablespoons brandy*
*1/2 cup dry white wine*
*1 1/2 to 2 cups chicken broth*
*3/4 cup diced carrot and onion together*
*1/2 cup rice*
*2/3 cup cream*
*cayenne pepper*

1) Season the lobster with the salt, pepper, parsley, thyme, and bay leaf. Melt 1/2 cup (8 tablespoons) of the butter in a pan large enough to accommodate the lobster; saute the pieces, turning occasionally, until the shells turn red–about 5 to 10 minutes.

2) Moisten the lobster with the brandy, ignite it briefly, and then add the wine. Reduce the liquid by two thirds. Add 1/2 cup of the chicken broth and the carrot and onion. Cook for 10 minutes. Remove the parsley, thyme, and bay leaf.

3) Cook the rice in 1 cup of the chicken broth. Set aside.

4) Take the lobster meat out of the shells and set aside for garnish.

5) Pound the shells in a mortar. Add the cooked rice and the liquid left from cooking the lobster. Put this mixture through a fine sieve into a 10-inch saucepan. Boil it briefly, adding chicken stock if necessary tomake 2 cups of sauce. Strain the sauce and keep warm in a *bain-marie*.

6) Add the lobster shells to the cooked rice and the liquid left from cooking the lobster.

7) Put this mixture through a fine sieve into a 10 inch saucepan. Boil briefly, adding more chicken broth if necessary to make 2 cups sauce.

8) Strain the sauce and keep warm in a *bain-marie*.

9) Cut the remaining butter (6 tablespoons) into 1/4-inch pieces and add them to the sauce gradually while stirring. Stir in the cream, and then the cayenne pepper.

10) Serve, covering hot pasta with lobster pieces as garnish.

### ARROSTO DI VITELLO RIPIENO
#### (Milk-Fed Veal Roast)

*2-pound boneless breast of milk-fed veal*
*4 pounds fresh spinach, cleaned thoroughly and coarsely*
*  chopped*
*1/2 cup grated Parmesan cheese*
*1 clove garlic, finely minced*
*1 pinch fresh rosemary*
*freshly-ground black pepper, to taste*
*2 carrots, cut into 1-inch pieces*
*2 small potatoes, cut into 1-inch cubes*
*2 onions, cut into 1-inch cubes*
*parsley, for garnish*

1) Preheat the oven to 350.

2) Spread out the veal roast and cover it with the spinach, parmesan, garlic, rosemary, and pepper. Roll the roast around the stuffing and secure it with string or pins.

3) Put the roast in a 12-inch buttered baking pan and surround it with the vegetables.

4) Roast the veal for 45 minutes until golden brown. Baste it at least once during roasting.

5) Serve the roast on a large platter, garnished with the cooked vegetables and the parsley. Each serving should be a 1 1/2-inch slice per person.

### LEGUMI VARI
(Mixed Vegetables)

*4 cups zucchini, sliced*
*4 cups fresh peas, shelled*
*4 cups fresh corn kernels*
*4 cups baby white onions, peeled*
*4 cups carrots, scraped and sliced*
*4 tablespoons butter*
*salt and pepper, to taste*

1) Cook each vegetable separately in 1 cup of boiling water for 3 to 4 minutes (nouvelle cuisine).

2) Mix the cooked vegetables in a large serving dish, toss with the butter, add the salt and pepper to taste, and serve.

### SORBETTO DI FRUTTA
(Sorbet with Fresh Fruits)

*2 quarts assorted sorbets (lemon, orange, strawberry, raspberry)*
*1 orange, peeled and cubed*
*1 pint strawberries, halved or quartered, depending on size*
*1 pint raspberries*
*2 bananas, sliced*
*1 pineapple, cubed*

In glass dessert dishes, surround a scoop of sorbet with pieces of the fresh fruit.

OUT OF MANY ONE PEOPLE

# THE EMBASSY OF JAMAICA

*Dinner for Six*

BANANA AND PINEAPPLE SALAD WITH LEMON FRENCH
DRESSING

SPICY PUMPKIN SOUP WITH GINGER

CURRIED CHICKEN

BAKED LOBSTER

COAT OF ARMS RICE AND BEANS

FRIED RIPE PLANTAIN

COCONUT CREAM


BEVERAGES

BLUE MOUNTAIN COFFEE
PONCHE DE CREME
SHANDY
PLANTER'S PUNCH

The azure-blue waters of the Caribbean, dazzling white beaches, reggae music, and the color and taste of tropical fruits and vegetables–all this is Jamaica. Next to being there, the best part of enjoying this beautiful Caribbean island is savoring the Jamaican foods in your local market: plump jumbo shrimp, fiery peppers, cherry tomatoes, melons, bananas, rum, chocolate and Blue Mountain coffee, all exotic and palate-pleasing. Jamaica is one of the most ravishingly beautiful, seductive islands in the tropics.

The Arawaks, the original inhabitants of the island, called their island Xaymaca, "land of wood and water," in homage to the majestic blue-green mountains thick with foliage: three thousand types of trees and plants, fruits and flowers, all watered by 126 rivers cascading down the mountainsides.

Noel Coward is just one of the many great and near great habitues of the island. He visited Jamaica in 1948 and built his house, Firefly, where he spent the last twenty-three years of his life. His guest book is filled with famous names, including Vivien Leigh and Ian Fleming. Coward himself is buried on a crest just behind his house.

Jamaican Ambassador H. E. Keith Johnson, a career diplomat who has served in West Germany, the Netherlands, Israel and New York City, and his wife Pamela, have shared with us some of the favorite dishes served at their sprawling terraced country house in Chevy Chase, Maryland, a suburb of Washington, D.C. There are flowers throughout the large sunny rooms, and statues and paintings of Jamaica. The drawing room, with its bright colors and plants, makes you feel as though you were enjoying a long cold drink on the island of Jamaica, even though there may be snow on the outside patio.

A spokesman at the embassy explained the current popularity of Jamaican cuisine. "Americans have had an interest in spicy regional cuisine for a number of years. Cajun and southern-style dishes have created a major impact on American dining preferences. Now, 'south-of-the-border' is taking on a new meaning: Caribbean cooking.

"This is a direct result of record numbers of people traveling to the Carribean, more local products becoming available in the U.S., and a growing interest in experimenting with new flavors."

So, while sipping a Planter's Punch, let's join in a Jamaican toast: "To Your Great Health."

## BANANA AND PINEAPPLE SALAD WITH LEMON FRENCH DRESSING

*6 ounces cheddar cheese*
*4 tablespoons pineapple juice*
*6 ripe bananas*
*12 leaves iceberg lettuce, or romaine*
*6 slices pineapple*
*LEMON FRENCH DRESSING (see below)*
*cherries, for garnish*


1) Grate the cheddar and add the pineapple juice. Beat until creamy.

2) Slice the bananas lengthwise and spread each piece with the cheese mixture. Also spread some of the mixture on the pineapple pieces.

3) Arrange two lettuce or romaine leaves on each of six plates. Put one pineapple slice and two banana pieces on each. Cover with LEMON DRESSING (see below) and garnish with cherries.


### LEMON FRENCH DRESSING

*3/4 cup salad oil*
*3/4 cup fresh lemon juice*
*3/4 teaspoon salt*
*2 tablespoons honey*
*1/8 teaspoon ground cayenne pepper*

Mix all the ingredients and shake well.

## SPICY PUMPKIN SOUP WITH GINGER

*2 pounds chuck roast, cut in 1-inch cubes*
*2 quarts water*
*1 large yam (1/2 pound), peeled and quartered*
*2 pounds fresh pumpkin pieces, peeled and free of seeds*
*2 scallions*
*1 clove garlic*
*1 hot green pepper*
*1 sprig fresh thyme or 1/8 teaspoon dried*
*salt to taste*
*1/2-inch piece ginger, grated*

1) Place the meat cubes in the water and boil them until almost cooked–about half an hour.

2) Put in the yam, pumpkin, scallions, garlic, hot pepper, and thyme. Let the soup boil for another half an hour, or until the pumpkin is soft.

3) Remove and discard the hot pepper, then puree the soup and return it to the pot.

4) Taste the soup and add salt if necessary. Add water if needed to make a consistency of heavy cream. Put in the grated ginger just before serving.

## CURRIED CHICKEN

3  2-pound chickens (fryers), cut up
salt and pepper to taste
3 tablespoons vegetable oil
2 cloves garlic, minced
4 scallions, chopped
1/2 teaspoon freshly-ground black pepper
2 tablespoons curry powder
1 tablespoon ground allspice
1 small piece ginger (1/2 by 1/4-inch), minced
2 cups coconut milk
3 potatoes, peeled and quartered
1 cup rice
2 cups water
1 teaspoon salt

1)  Put the chicken pieces into a 4-quart saucepan, add salt and pepper to taste, and pour in water to cover.  Bring it to a boil, reduce the heat, and simmer until the chicken is cooked, about 30 minutes.  Cool slightly and remove the bones and skin.

2)  Heat the oil in a 14-inch skillet and add the garlic, scallions, pepper, curry, allspice and ginger.  Cook for 5 minutes over medium heat, then add the chicken.  Simmer over low heat for 5 minutes.  Make sure all the chicken comes in contact with the spice mixture.  Add the coconut milk and potatoes.  Cover and cook over low heat for 30 minutes or until the potatoes are tender all the way through.  Turn off the heat.

3)  While the chicken and potatoes are cooking, prepare the rice. Heat the rice, water, and salt to a boil.  Stir it, then reduce the heat, cover, and simmer for 14 minutes without stirring or lifting the cover.  Remove the pot from the heat, lightly fluff the rice, cover it again and let stand for 5 more minutes.

4) Serve the chicken with the steamed rice and mango chutney on the side.

### BAKED LOBSTER

2 pounds freshly-cooked lobster meat (for instructions on how to
  cook live lobster, see the recipes from the Chinese Embassy)
5 tablespoons fresh lime juice
7 1/2 ounces butter
4 ounces onion, finely chopped
1 teaspoon garlic, crushed
1 teaspoon chopped hot chilis
1 1/2 ounces white bread crumbs (remove crusts before
crumbling)
1 teaspoon Worcestershire sauce
salt and pepper to taste

1) Check over the lobster meat for pieces of shell and cartilage.
Cut it into 1-inch chunks and put it into a deep bowl with the
lime juice, coating all the pieces thoroughly. Set aside to
marinate for 15 minutes.

2) Melt 2 ounces of the butter in a large, heavy frying pan. Add
the onion, garlic, and chilis, and cook over medium heat until
the onion is transparent–about 5 minutes. Put in 1 ounce of the
bread crumbs and cook, stirring, until they are toasted to a
delicate brown.

3) Add the marinated lobster meat and its juice, and 2 ounces of
butter. Keep at moderate heat until the butter is melted, and
then turn off the heat. Toss the ingredients. Add the
Worcestershire sauce, and salt and pepper to taste.

4) Preheat the oven to 375.

5) Butter the bottom and sides of a 1 1/2-pint baking dish with 1/2 ounce of the butter. You may soften it and spread it or melt it and use a pastry brush.

6) Transfer the lobster meat to the baking dish, distributing it evenly. Sprinkle the remaining 1/2 ounce of bread crumbs on top. Dot the casserole with the remaining 3 ounces of butter, cut into 1/4-inch pieces. Bake it for 15 minutes or until the bread crumbs are lightly browned. Serve at once.

### FRIED RIPE PLANTAIN

*2 plantains, ripe but not soft*
*salt and pepper to taste*
*1/2 cup flour*
*1/2 cup bread crumbs*
*1/2 cup corn oil*
*1/2 cup brown sugar*

1) Slice the plantains lengthwise. Sprinkle them with salt and pepper.

2) Dip them first into the flour, then the bread crumbs. Heat the oil and fry the plaintain slices at medium heat.

3) Sprinkle one side with 1/4 cup of the sugar and cook until golden brown. Then flip them and fry on the other side, sprinkling with the remaining sugar. It should take about 10 minutes to cook them.

4) Serve the plaintains hot or cool.

---

## COAT OF ARMS RICE AND BEANS

*1 cup red kidney beans*
*1 quart coconut milk*
*2 scallions*
*1 sprig thyme, or 1 bay leaf*
*1 clove garlic, crushed*
*3 teaspoons salt*
*1 tablespoon sugar*
*3 cups rice*

1) To prepare the beans, put them in a pot with water to cover and a little to spare. Bring to a boil, cook for 2 minutes, cover, and let stand (off the heat) for an hour.

2) Put the coconut milk in a 4-quart pan and add the soaked beans. Cook until the beans are almost tender–about 1 hour. Test the beans. They should not be overcooked.

3) Add the scallions, thyme, garlic, salt, sugar, and rice to the pot. Cook over low heat, stirring once or twice, until the rice is well cooked. It should take about an hour for the water to evaporate. If the mixture looks dry before that time, add more water.

## COCONUT CREAM

*1 package unflavored gelatin*
*2 cups coconut milk*
*1 8-ounce can sweetened condensed milk*
*1/2 teaspoon salt*
*1 teaspoon nutmeg*

1) Mix the gelatin into 1/4 cup of the coconut milk.

2) Add 1/2 cup more coconut milk. Stir over low heat until the gelatin is dissolved.

3) Add the remaining coconut milk, the condensed milk, and the salt and stir until dissolved. Strain the mixture.

4) Pour the cream into individual containers, such as ramekins; sprinkle them with nutmeg and put them into the refrigerator to set.

## BEVERAGES

### PONCHE DE CREME

*3 eggs*
*grated peel of 1/2 lime*
*1/2 pint rum*
*1 can sweetened condensed milk*
*1 can evaporated milk*
*pinch of salt*
*1/4 teaspoon nutmeg*
*dash of bitters*

Beat the eggs with the lime peel. Add the other ingredients. Bottle the mixture, chill it, and serve it over cracked ice.

### SHANDY

Combine equal parts ginger beer and lager beer. Serve the drink in a shallow-bowl champagne glass with a short straw.

### PLANTER'S PUNCH

*12 ounces dark rum*
*6 tablespoons Karo syrup*
*6 tablespoons lime juice*
*orange, pineapple, and lemon slices, for garnish*
*mint sprigs, for garnish*

For each drink, stir 2 ounces of rum, 1 tablespoon of syrup, and 1 tablespoon of lime juice into a tall glass filled with crushed ice. Garnish with fruit slices and mint sprigs.

# THE EMBASSY OF JAPAN

*Popular Japanese Dishes*

## SUNUMONO
*(Celery and Shrimp in Vinegar Dressing)*

## OKONOMI-YAKI
*(Japanese Pancakes)*

## TEMPURA
*(Deep-Fried Fish and Vegetables)*

## JAGAIMO TO GYUNIKU NO NIMONO
*(Potatoes with Beef)*

## TONKATSU
*(Deep-Fried Pork Cutlets)*

## TAKIKOMI
*(Flavored Rice Mix)*

## ORANGE SHERBET

## BEVERAGES

COCKTAILS
WINE
SAKE
SUNTORY, ASAHI, SAPPORO, AND KIRIN BEER
TEA

# JAPAN

The recently-built residence of the Japanese Ambassador to the United States, His Excellency Nobuo Matsunaga, appears suspended in the air above acres of beautifully-cultivated gardens bordered with Japanese cherry blossoms. Floor-to-ceiling windows flood the large rooms with sunlight by day, and by night gold chandeliers with tiny bulbs provide a starlit brilliance. Thick, pale-blue rugs with pink and gold designs cover the floor of the long drawing room, which overlooks a pond fed by a waterfall and surrounded by red, green, and gold shrubbery. A picturesque white-roofed teahouse sits across from the waterfall. The delicate beauty of this Japanese artistry makes this embassy one of the most scenic in Washington.

An appreciation of the glories of nature is reflected in Japanese dining as well as in decor. The four seasons of the year inspire menus just as they do art works. Spring (March to May) covers the mountains and gardens with pink cherry blossoms, and brings to the table tender young bamboo shoots. Summer (June to August) begins with the rainy rice-planting season, followed by sunny days and opening festivals at beaches and mountain resorts. Everyone eats *ayu*, a fresh-water fish. Autumn (September to November) brings a riot of colorful foliage in the mountains, where bright chrysanthemums and pine mushrooms grow. Pine mushrooms are featured as a tribute to fall. Winter (December to February) finds everyone skiing and skating in the crisp air, and then dining on *fugu*, a spiny blowfish that is supposedly an aphrodisiac.

The Japanese concentrate on beautiful and intricate food presentations. They pride themselves on the artistic touches given to *sushi* and *sashimi*, and to the golden *tempura*. This last is a fish course introduced to Japan in the seventeenth century by Portuguese Jesuit missionaries in Nagasaki. They used the Portuguese word "tempura" for the days on which they abstained from meat. Later in that century, the Chinese added deep-frying techniques and a recipe for shellfish batter; the tempura enjoyed throughout the world today is made with vegetables as well as fish.

Dinner at the Japanese Embassy is an elegant affair with five to ten courses, each dish a colorful decorative work of art and a unique delicacy. Chef Saito from Osaka created his finest display in early 1986 for the visit of Prince Hiro, first son of the Crown Prince of Japan.

The recipes in this chapter were furnished by the Embassy of Japan through the courtesy of Toshiko Sunada and Ayao Okumura of AJiCommunications. Each dish serves six people.

They are very popular Japanese dishes and may be combined in various ways to make a gracious dinner. *Tempura* for example is usually featured at all dinners at the Japanese Embassy. The Japanese hope that you will enjoy these "favorite recipes" from Japan.

Several beverages accompany an important Japanese dinner. Before the meal, guests gather in the reception hall, where they are served beer, cocktails, or fruit juice. During the meal, warm sake is served in small, beautifully-decorated cups. Beer is also served; Suntory, Asahi, Sapporo and Kirin are the beers the Japanese produce domestically.

During the meal, the host toasts the guests of honor as he lifts his glass, bows, and says "Kam Pai,"..."Bottoms Up." The guests return the toast, compliment each other, and bow. The toasts go around the table until everyone has joined in at least once.

## SUNUMONO
### (Celery and Shrimp in Vinegar Dressing)

*3/4 pound cleaned and deveined small shrimp (fresh, or frozen)*
*1 tablespoon sesame seeds*
*6-8 stalks celery*
*2 tablespoons rice vinegar*
*1 tablespoon soy suace*
*1 tablespoon sugar*
*1 tablespoon water*

1) If you are using fresh shrimp, peel them and make a shallow cut lengthwise down the back of each one; remove the black vein. Wash the shrimp, then drop them into boiling salted water. Cover the pot, return it to the boil, and simmer for 4-6 minutes. Drain the shrimp and refrigerate until ready to use. If you are using frozen shrimp, drop them into boiling salted water for 1-2 minutes, then drain and refrigerate. For canned shrimp, simply drain.

2) Toast the sesame seeds in an ungreased skillet over medium heat, stirring for about 2 minutes or until golden.

3) Remove the strings from the celery; cut the stalks into 1/2-inch pieces, then cut these vertically into thin sticks. There should be about 2 1/2 cups of sticks.

4) Drop the celery sticks into rapidly boiling water for just a moment, then remove and cool them in ice water. After 2-3 minutes, drain the celery and squeeze out any excess water. Combine the celery with the cooked shrimp in a glass bowl.

5) Mix the vinegar, soy sauce, sugar, and water, and pour this dressing over the shrimp and celery. Toss the salad, cover it, and refrigerate it for an hour.

6) When ready to serve, remove the salad to lettuce-lined bowls with a slotted spoon. Sprinkle it with the toasted sesame seeds and serve.

## OKONOMI-YAKI
(Japanese Pancakes)

2 1/4 cups flour
1/4 teaspoon salt
1/2 teaspoon monosodium glutamate
3/4 teaspoon baking powder
1 cup soup stock or milk
3 cups cabbage, shredded
1 1/2 cups cooked beef or pork, chopped into small pieces
9 tablespoons Worcestershire sauce
3 tablespoons tomato ketchup
1 1/2 teaspoons whiskey
6 eggs
6 mushrooms, thinly sliced
1-2 tablespoons vegetable oil

1) To make the pancake batter, mix the flour, salt, monosodium glutamate, and baking powder and sift them into a large bowl. Gradually add the soup stock or milk.

2) Divide the cabbage and meat into six portions and place each in a small bowl.

3) Make the sauce by mixing the Worcestershire sauce, ketchup, and whiskey. Set aside.

4) Put an equal amount of the batter into each of the six bowls. Break an egg into each bowl, and mix the egg and the batter with a spoon.

5) Cook the pancakes one at a time over high heat in a greased 6-inch skillet. The pan should be hot but not smoking when the batter is poured in, and the pancake should be less than 1/2-inch thick. Place the mushrooms on top of the batter. When the pancake is 60 percent cooked, fry the other side. When it is cooked through, turn it again, top it with the sauce, and put it on a serving plate.

### TEMPURA
(Deep-Fried Fish and Vegetables)

12 shrimp, with tails, peeled and deveined
1/2 pound white fish filets, cut into bite-size pieces
1/2 pound scallops, halved
1 cup sliced carrots (1/4-inch pieces)
1 1/2 cups cauliflower florets
1 cup green bean pieces (2-inch), blanched
1 cup green onion pieces (2-inch)
1 green pepper, cut into 1/4-inch rings
1 medium onion, sliced and separated into rings
1 potato, boiled and cut into 1/4-inch slices
2 or more cups vegetable oil (peanut, safflower, or soybean)

*BATTER:*

2 eggs, beaten
1 cup ice water
3/4 cup all-purpose flour
1 tablespoon cornstarch
1/2 teaspoon baking powder
1/2 teaspoon salt

*DIPPING SAUCE:*

1/4 cup chicken broth
1/4 cup cold water
1/4 cup soy sauce
1 teaspoon sugar

1) Make four crosswise slits on the undersides of the shrimp to prevent curling as they are deep-fried. Pat the seafood and vegetables dry if necessary, then cover and refrigerate them until cooking time.

2) Pour oil to a depth of 1 to 1 1/2 inches into a wok or very deep frying pan. Heat it to 360 degrees.

3) While the oil is heating, mix the batter ingredients with a fork until blended. The mixture will be thin and lumpy.

4) Dip the seafood and vegetable pieces into the batter with tongs, a fork, or chopsticks. Allow the excess batter to drip into a bowl. Fry a few pieces at a time (so that the oil will remain hot), turning them once, until they are golden brown–about 2 to 3 minutes.

5) Using tongs, place the deep-fried tempura on a draining tray to remove excess oil.

6) Mix all the ingredients for the dipping sauce and heat until warm. Arrange the seafood and vegetable on a serving platter and serve with the warm sauce.

## JAGAIMO TO GYUNIKU NO NIMONO
### (Potatoes With Beef)

*1 pound lean beef, thinly sliced and cut into 4-inch lengths*
*1 pound medium potatoes*
*1 pound onions*
*3/4 cup beef bouillon*
*2 tablespoons vegetable oil*
*1 cup water*
*4 tablespoons sake*
*6 tablespoons sugar*
*6 tablespoons soy sauce*

1) Freeze the meat strips for 1 hour. (This will make them crisp when fried.)

2) Wash, peel, and quarter the potatoes; boil them for 10 minutes or until tender.

3) Peel and halve the onions and cut into 1/2-inch sections. Boil them in the bouillon for a minute; drain them, reserving the liquid.

4) Heat a 4-inch deep, heavy pot over high heat and then add the oil and heat it until hot but not smoking. Add the meat strips and fry them briefly. Add 1/4 cup of the reserved bouillon liquid, the water, and the sake.

5) When these ingredients begin to boil, scoop off any fat floating on the top. Add the cooked potatoes, onions, sugar, and soy sauce. Cover the pot and simmer over medium heat until 1/4 of the liquid remains–about 15 minutes.

## TONKATSU
### (Deep-Fried Pork Cutlets)

*6 pork cutlets, about 1/2-inch thick*
*salt and freshly-ground black pepper to taste*
*1 1/2 cups flour*
*2 eggs, beaten lightly*
*1 cup bread crumbs*
*1-2 cups vegetable oil*
*3/4 pound cabbage*
*1 bunch parsley, for garnish*
*Worcestershire sauce, as an accompaniment (optional)*

1) Trim the fat from the cutlets, season them with salt and pepper, and let them stand for 3 minutes.  Then dredge them in the flour, dip them in the beaten eggs, and roll them in the bread crumbs.  Set them aside for 3 minutes, or until the bread crumbs are moist.

2) Shred the cabbage and place it in chilled water for 5-6 minutes.  Drain it and pile it on a serving platter.

3) Pour the oil into a deep 12-inch skillet to a depth of 3/4-inch and heat it to 360, or until it is hot but not smoking.  Deep-fry the breaded cutlets for a total of 4 minutes, or until golden brown on both sides.

4) Place the hot cutlets onto the shredded cabbage, and garnish with the parsley.  Serve with Worcestershire sauce as an accompaniment.

## TAKIKOMI
### (Flavored Rice Mix)

*1/4 pound Shiitake (or any available) mushrooms, thinly sliced*
*2 carrots, chopped*
*1/2 pound cooked chicken, cut into 1/2-inch cubes*
*1 tablespoon vegetable oil*
*3 cups California rice*
*3 1/2 cups water*
*4 tablespoons soy sauce*
*1 tablespoon sake*
*1/2 tablespoon sugar*
*1 bunch parsley, for garnish*

1) Boil the mushroom slices briefly in water to cover, and then drain them thoroughly.

2) Steam the carrot pieces for about 3-5 minutes, until just tender.

3) Saute the chicken, the mushrooms, and the carrots in the oil over medium heat for several minutes, until the pieces are coated with oil and browned lightly.

4) Transfer the sauteed ingredients to an electric rice cooker and mix in the rice, water, soy sauce, sake, and sugar. Level out the mixture so that the top is flat. Cover the cooker and turn it on low for about 40 minutes, or until the cooker (if automatic) turns itself off. Wait 10 minutes before removing the lid. Mix the rice well, arrange it on a large serving dish, and garnish it with the parsley.

5) In the absence of an automatic rice cooker, cook all the ingredients on low heat for about 40 minutes.

# THE EMBASSY OF MEXICO

*Dinner for Eight*

## SALSA VERDE
*(Green Sauce Dip)*

## GUACAMOLE
*(Avocado Dip)*

## CREMA DE CALABACITAS
*(Cream of Zucchini Soup)*

## ENSALADA DE NOPALES
*(Nopal Cactus Salad)*

## PESCADO CON ALCAPARRAS
*(Haddock With Capers)*

## CAPIROTADA
*(Bread Pudding)*

## BEVERAGE

## TECATE
*(Mexican Beer, Served with Lime and Salt)*

# MEXICO

Mexico–the name suggests color, romance, excitement and history. From the mystique of Mexico's ancient past–the pyramids and ancient temples honoring the Aztec and Mayan Gods, the old Moorish mansions, and the ornate Baroque cathedrals built by the sixteenth century Spanish conquistadors–to today's sandy beaches, flowering courtyards, elegant haciendas, Spanish guitars, and whirling red-sequined skirts, Mexico may well be the most colorful country in the world.

Mexican food is equally bright and eye-catching, featuring spicy red, yellow, and green jalapeno peppers, avocados, and multicolored fruits and vegetables found in the open food markets.

Surprisingly, the exterior of the Mexican Embassy shows none of this south-of-the-border brilliance. It is a staid, beige brick mansion on 16th Street, Washington's second Embassy Row. Originally built as a French townhouse at the end of the nineteenth century, it was purchased by the Mexican Government in 1921.

It is only once you step inside that you encounter the real, colorful Mexico. From the first floor of the huge open lobby, up the winding staircase to the skylit fourth floor, there is a floor-to-ceiling panorama of brilliant, vivid Mexican murals by Roberto Cueva Del Rio. The paintings are a wonderland of movement and color illustrating Mexican life and history. There are larger-than-life, dramatically-dressed people working and playing, gold-encrusted portraits of the Spanish conquerers and Moorish kings, polychromatic scenes of lakes and mountains including Mexico's two great volcanos, Popocateptl and Ixtacihuatl, and depictions of the original Aztec Indians done in brilliant reds, yellows and browns.

There is a spacious music room on the second level, with gold-leaf walls decorated with French fleur-de-lys, an enormous gold pipe organ, and a grand piano.

The dining room, where Mexican Ambassador Espinosa de los Reyes and his wife, Sofia, entertain a large community of

Mexican friends and Washington dignitaries, is the largest in Washington--thirty-three by forty feet. It is of a very formal Renaissance style, with walls and columns in soft white.

The menu and recipes included here were put together by the ambassador's staff, with the assistance of Chef Jose Prud'homme of the Restaurant Cinco de Mayo in New York. Enjoy these Mexican specialties with a glass of Tecate, a light Mexican beer; it is traditionally served ice cold in a salt-rimmed glass, and followed by a bite into a slice of lime. "A Tu Salud"..."To Your Health!

### SALSA VERDE
(Green Sauce Dip)

*1/2 pound tomatillos, peeled (a green tomato available in
   markets specializing in Mexican food)*
*3 serrano chilis*
*1 medium clove garlic*
*1/4 medium white onion*
*1 tablespoon coriander, roughly chopped*
*1/4 teaspoon salt*
*1 pinch sugar*
*8 tortillas*

1) Remove the paper-thin skin from the tomatillos and boil them in just enough water to cover.  Cook until they change color from green to yellow--about 15 minutes.  Drain them and reserve the water.

2) In a blender, puree the tomatillos with the remaining ingredients until almost smooth.  Add 1/2 cup of the reserved water and continue blending until the sauce is as thick as heavy cream.

3) Serve this as a dip with warmed tortilla chips, or put the sauce inside the tortillas and roll tightly.

### GUACAMOLE
(Avocado Dip)

*4 very ripe medium-size avocados, peeled and mashed*
*2 small onions, finely chopped*
*1 4-ounce can green jalapeno peppers, peeled and finely chopped*
*2 tablespoons lime juice*
*salt to taste*
*1/2 teaspoon ground coriander*
*1 large tomato, chopped fine*

1)  Mix everything but the tomato in a large bowl, with a fork. Stir in the tomato gently.

2)  Serve with warmed tortilla chips.

## CREMA DE CALABACITAS
### (Cream of Zucchini Soup)

*2 pounds very tender zucchini, chopped in 1/2-inch pieces*
*1 medium onion, chopped*
*1/2 pound tomatoes, chopped*
*1 cup chicken bouillon*
*1 cup heavy cream*
*2 cups milk*
*salt and pepper to taste*

1) Season the zucchini with some salt, and put it into a pan with the onion, tomato, and bouillon.  Bring the mixture to a boil, and cook for 3 minutes.  Remove the pan from the heat and let it stand for 5 minutes.

2) Stir in the cream and the milk gradually; add more salt and the pepper.  Bring to a low boil, stirring, and simmer for 15 minutes over low heat.

3)  The soup may be served hot or cold.

### ENSALADA DE NOPALES
(Nopal Cactus Salad)

*2 pounds fresh nopal cactus (see note below)*
   *or 1 32-ounce can Nopales al Natural, drained and rinsed*
*3 tablespoons wine vinegar*
*salt and pepper to taste*
*1/4 cup olive oil*
*1 teaspoon oregano*
*1 pound tomatoes, chopped into 1/4-inch pieces*
*1 medium onion, chopped into 1/4-inch pieces*
*1/2 cup fresh coriander, chopped*
*1 avocado (preferably Hass), peeled and sliced*
*1 tomato, sliced*
*1 onion, separated into rings*
*2 ounces white Mexican cheese (Queso Blanco), crumbled*

1) In a large bowl, combine the cactus, vinegar, salt and pepper, oil, and oregano.

2) Add the chopped tomatoes, chopped onion, and the coriander. Mix well, and let marinate for at least 15 minutes.

3) Serve on a platter garnished with the sliced avocado, the sliced tomato, and the onion rings. Top with the crumbled cheese.

Note: If using fresh cactus, remove the thorns with a sharp knife without peeling the skin. Cut the cactus into 1/4 by 1 1/2-inch pieces. Boil them with 1/4 teaspoon of baking soda for 1/2 hour or until tender. Rinse the cactus, drain it, and let it cool.

### PESCADO CON ALCAPARRAS
(Haddock With Capers)

*2 pounds haddock, or any white fish*
*salt and pepper to taste*
*1/4 cup olive oil*
*1 large spanish onion, chopped*
*2 medium cloves garlic, chopped*
*2 tablespoons whole capers*
*1/2 pound tomatoes, chopped*
*1 bunch fresh coriander, chopped very fine*
*1/2 teaspoon oregano*
*1 shredded jalapeno pepper*
*1 lemon, sliced, for garnish*

1) Salt and pepper the haddock and poach it in an 8-inch pan in an inch of water for 5 minutes. Set aside.

2) In a flameproof 8-inch pan, combine the olive oil, onion, garlic, capers, and tomatoes, and saute until lightly browned– about 5 minutes.

3) Remove the pan from the heat and add the coriander, oregano, and salt and pepper if desired.

4) Place the fish in the pan and sprinkle with the jalapeno. Cover and simmer for 15 minutes.

5) Serve the fish on a large platter, garnish with the lemon slices.

## CAPIROTADA
### (Bread Pudding)

3 loaves unseeded Italian bread
2 1/2 pounds packed raw brown sugar (Piloncillo)
2 quarts water
rind of 2 oranges, grated very fine
rind of 1 lime, grated very fine
8 cloves
1-inch piece stick cinnamon
1 cup raisins
1/2 cup slivered almonds
2/3 cup candied citron, chopped
1 pound white cheese (Queso Blanco or Monterey Jack),
    crumbled

1) Preheat the oven to 450.

2) Cut off the ends of the bread, and slice the rest into 1/4-inch pieces.

3) Place the bread pieces on a cooling rack over a baking sheet and toast, turning once, until golden brown–about 10 to 15 minutes each side.

4) To make the syrup, combine the brown sugar, water, orange and lime rind, cloves, and cinnamon in a 3-quart saucepan. Boil for 15 minutes and let cool slightly.

5) To make the filling, combine the raisins, almonds, citron, and cheese in a bowl.

6) Reset the oven temperature to 350.

7) Butter an 8 by 8 by 2-inch baking dish. Soak each slice of bread in the syrup for a few seconds. Make layers of the soaked bread and the filling in the baking dish, beginning with the bread and ending with the filling.

8) Bake the pudding for 35 minutes.

# THE EMBASSY OF THE KINGDOM OF MOROCCO

*Dinner for Six*

## BASTELA
*(Chicken Pie)*

## ZEILOOK
*(Eggplant Salad)*

## DJAJ M'KALLI
*(Chicken with Lemon and Olives)*

## H'RIRA
*(Ramadan Soup)*

## COUSCOUS

## CORNES DE GAZELLES
*(Almond Gazelle Horns)*

Morocco, the exotic kingdom of Hassan II, is a land of mystery and intrigue. Located on the sand-swept Sahara, its coastlines are the sun-drenched beaches of the Mediterranean. Its cities–Casablanca, Marrakesh, Rabat, and Fez, with their Casbahs, Souks, rugs, and mint tea–are a fantasy come true.

Morocco is a Muslim world; religion and government are one. There are royal palaces, veiled women, Roman ruins, holy men, snake charmers, belly dancers, and camels, all mixed with the trapppings of luxury–elegant hotels, brilliant jewels, leather, silks, and Mercedes Benz.

But nowhere is the magic so immediately and impressively manifest as in the food; the Moroccan meal is always a ceremony. Guests are seated on cushions around a low table and given hot damp towels before the food is served. These are used to wash the fingers of the right hand, which are used in place of knives and forks.

After reciting the ritual "Bismillah" ("praise be to God"), each diner partakes of the meal from a common dish. The meat is always well done, and it is customary for the host to offer his guests the finest cuts. To refuse this preferential treatment is a breach of etiquette. The meal consists of a procession of succulent dishes and can last up to four hours.

Morocco's national dish is *couscous*; the word refers both to the stew itself and to the durum-wheat semolina that is the principle ingredient. The stew is a savory mixture of mutton or chicken, vegetables, chick peas, and raisins.

Two other great favorites among Moroccans are *bastela*, a flaky pastry pie stuffed with chicken or pigeon and almonds, and *tajine*, a sweet spicy stew of mutton or poultry, olives, almonds, prunes, and lemons. Another "must" is *h'rira*, a thick soup made with bite-size pieces of meat, lots of lentils, and chick peas or beans. Moroccan pastries are often rich with honey and almonds. Gazelle horns, included in the menu to follow, are certainly the most typical and popular.

The Moroccan national drink, enjoyed by rich and poor at all times of the day and night, is green tea flavored with fresh mint.

# KINGDOM OF MOROCCO

Served in small glasses with plenty of sugar, it is sometimes seasoned with orange blossoms. Almond juice, another favorite beverage, is made with orange blossom syrup. And for important guests, a typical symbol of hospitality is the offer of milk, accompanied by dates.

The recipes given here were furnished by His Excellency Ambassador Maati Jorio, and Madame Jorio. They are a handsome couple, full of enthusiasm for America and for Washington, D. C., their fifth posting after Moscow, Bucharest, Madrid, and Tripoli. Madame Jorio supervises the elaborate meals served at the elegant embassy, planning the menus and passing them on to Ms. Sethia Smaq, the executive chef. Ms. Smaq, at 25, is one of the youngest and prettiest of Washington's chefs. She has had great experience in preparing Moroccan dishes, and was trained in the Ecole de Hoteliere in Rabat, the capitol of Morocco.

Parties in the lavish residence, with its beautiful Moroccan rugs and gold and silver samovars, are a wonderfully stylish experience.

In Morocco, the toast is "To Your Very Good Health"... "Be'saaha."

## BASTELA
(Chicken Pie)

1 medium-size chicken, skinned
salt to taste
2 cups parsley, chopped
2 pounds onions, grated
1/2 teaspoon pepper
1 teaspoon saffron powder
1 teaspoon cinnamon
1 tablespoon butter
2 cups water
1 tablespoon butter
4 large eggs, well beaten
2 tablespoons vegetable oil
1/4 cup almonds, skinned and chopped
1/2 cup sugar
1-2 tablespoons melted butter
1 package frozen phyllo dough or strudel leaves
1 egg yolk, lightly beaten
2 tablespoons powdered sugar

1) Place the whole chicken in a 12-inch saucepan with the salt, parsley, onions, pepper, saffron, and cinnamon. Cover with the 2 cups of water and cook over medium heat, stirring occasionally, until the chicken is tender; about 45 minutes.

2) Take the chicken out of the pan and cut it into 1/2-inch chunks, removing the bones. Pour off any remaining water in the pan and add the butter, then the eggs. Stir. When the eggs are set, remove the pan from the heat and stir in the chicken.

3) In a separate saucepan, heat the oil to hot but not smoking, and fry the almonds until golden brown, about 5 minutes. Mix them with the sugar and then add this to the chicken and egg mixture.

4) Preheat the oven to 325.

5) Brush a 10-inch Pyrex pie pan with melted butter and place a sheet of phyllo dough onto the pan so that it hangs over the edges. Brush this with more melted butter and repeat with another sheet of phyllo. Repeat this procedure until you have four to six layers of dough, depending on the desired thickness of crust.

6) Spread the chicken mixture into the pie pan. Cover it with a sheet of phyllo and brush this with butter. Continue as above for four to six layers of phyllo. Trim all the overhanging sheets of phyllo to within an inch of the pie plate. Brush the layers with the egg yolk and fold them under neatly. Brush the top of the pie with the remaining melted butter. Bake for 20 minutes, until golden brown, then dust with powdered sugar and serve.

## ZEILOOK
### (Eggplant Salad)

*2 pounds eggplant*
*salt to taste*
*1/2 cup olive oil*
*3 ripe tomatoes, peeled, seeded, and chopped*
*3 cloves garlic, chopped*
*1/2 teaspoon ground cumin*
*1 teaspoon sweet paprika*
*1 tablespoon fresh coriander, chopped*
*3 tablespoons fresh lemon juice*

1)  Peel three vertical strips of skin from each eggplant, leaving them striped.  Cut the eggplant horizontally into 1/2-inch slices. Salt the slices well and set them in a colander in the sink to drain for 30 minutes.  Then rinse them well, squeeze out excess moisture, and pat them dry with a paper towel.

2)  In a 12-inch skillet, heat the oil and fry the eggplant slices over low heat until browned on both sides.  Remove the slices with a slotted spoon, reserving the oil.  Mash the eggplant with the tomatoes, garlic, cumin, paprika, and coriander until the mixture is pureed.

3)  Fry the puree in the reserved oil for 20 minutes, or until most of the excess liquid has evaporated.  Turn the heat to low and continue frying for another 15 minutes, stirring often to prevent scorching.  Pour off the remaining oil and season to taste with the lemon juice.

4)  Serve the salad warm or cool.  It can be kept 3 or 4 days, covered, in a cool place.

### DJAJ M'KALLI
(Chicken with Lemon and Olives)

*2 chickens, halved*
*3 teaspoons salt*
*8 cloves garlic, crushed*
*3/4 cup vegetable oil*
*2 teaspoons powdered ginger*
*1 teaspoon turmeric*
*1 teaspoon freshly-ground black pepper*
*1 pinch saffron*
*2 medium onions, grated*
*1/4 pound unsalted butter*
*1/2 pound Greek olives (kalamata), pitted and well-rinsed*
*2 PICKLED LEMONS (see following page)*

1) To allow time for marinating, start this recipe a day ahead, or early in the day. Clean the halved chickens and remove the bones, skin, and fat. Rub them with a mixture of 2 teaspoons of the salt and six of the garlic cloves. Place them in a large deep saucepan, cover them with water, and let stand for 1 hour.

2) Remove the chicken halves and rub them with a mixture of the oil, ginger, turmeric, black pepper, saffron, and remaining salt. Allow them to marinate in the refrigerator for a few hours, or, if possible, overnight.

3) To cook the chicken, cut it into individual portions, place them in a 12-inch pot, and add the onions, butter, remaining garlic, and 1 quart water. Bring to a boil, then simmer for 20 minutes, until tender.

4) Wash the brine off the two PICKLED LEMONS and add them and the olives to the chicken. Cook another 5 minutes. Remove the chicken and boil down the liquid until it is thick.

5) Return the chicken to the pot and reheat just before serving.

### PICKLED LEMONS
(This recipe must be made at least 2 weeks before using)

*lemons*
*salt*
*1 glass or stoneware jar with tight lid*

Use as many lemons as will fit snugly in your jar. Cut off one end of each, then make two perpendicular cuts downward from this end almost all the way through, so that the lemon is divided into four attached wedges. Rub salt into the lemons and pack them in the jar. Let them stand for at least 2 weeks at room temperature. They should last up to 6 months.

## H'RIRA
### (Ramadan Soup)

*1/2 pound beef or lamb, cut into 1/4-inch cubes*
*1/4 pound dry chick peas, soaked overnight*
*2 medium onions, chopped*
*1/4 teaspoon salt*
*1/2 teaspoon freshly-ground black pepper*
*6 cups water*
*1/4 cup lentils*
*1/2 cup rice, rinsed*
*4 tomatoes, peeled, mashed, and drained*
*1 bunch parsley, finely chopped*
*1 bunch coriander, finely chopped*
*2 tablespoons all-purpose flour*
*1/2 teaspoon baking powder*
*1/2 cup warm water*
*fresh lemon juice to taste*

1) Put the meat, chick peas, onions, salt, and pepper in a 1-gallon pot with the 6 cups of water. Cook over medium heat for 25 minutes.

2) Add the lentils, rice, tomatoes, parsley, and coriander; bring to a boil over medium heat and cook for 15 minutes, uncovered.

3) After 15 minutes, lower the heat, cover the pot, and simmer the soup until the rice and lentils are cooked, about another 30 minutes.

4) While the soup is cooking, mix the flour and baking soda in the warm water and stir until free of lumps; set aside.

5) When everything is cooked, stir in the flour mixture. Add the fresh lemon juice to taste and serve warm.

## COUSCOUS

*1/2 cup butter*
*1 1/2 pounds lamb (shoulder cutlets), cut into 1/2-inch cubes*
  *or 1 1/2 pounds beef (round roast), cut into 1/2-inch cubes*
*1/4 cup dry chick peas, soaked overnight*
*1/4 pound onions, chopped*
*6 cups warm water*
*1/2 teaspoon saffron powder*
*1/4 teaspoon salt*
*1/2 teaspoon black pepper*
*1 1/2 pounds couscous (available in health food stores)*
*3 medium-size carrots, peeled and cut lengthwise into 4 strips*
*3 turnips, peeled and cut lengthwise into 3 pieces*
*3 medium zucchini, cut in half lengthwise*
*1 pound tomatoes, halved*
*1/4 cup seedless raisins*
*1 bunch coriander, finely chopped*
*1/2 pound yellow squash, cut in 1/2-inch slices*
*1 tablespoon butter*

Special Equipment; a *couscoussiere* (available in gourmet shops or large department stores), or a Dutch oven 12 inches in diameter and 10 inches deep, with a round open top into which a regular colander fits tightly.

1) Heat the butter in the bottom of the *couscoussiere* or in the Dutch oven; lightly brown the meat over medium heat for about 15 minutes. Drain off the fat and add the chick peas, onions, 6 cups of water, saffron powder, salt, and pepper.

2) Soak the couscous in warm water until the grains double in size—about 4 minutes. Then place it in the top part of the *couscoussiere* or in the colander (if the holes are too big, line the colander with cheesecloth). Fit the top part into the bottom part containing the browned meat. Cook over medium heat for 30 minutes. This will both cook the meat and steam the couscous.

3) Remove the top of the *coucoussiere* or the colander, and add all the vegetables, and the raisins, to the meat. Mix lightly, then replace the top part. Allow the couscous to steam for another 30 minutes while the vegetables cook. When done, the couscous will be soft but not mushy, and a bit firm to the touch.

4) Cooking time may vary depending on how firm one prefers the vegetables. Add extra water to the broth if necessary to make a total of 2 cups.

5) To serve, mix a tablespoon of butter into the couscous and pile it into the center of a large serving plate. Make an indentation in the couscous dome and put in the meat. Place the vegetables in an artistic arrangement around the couscous and the meat. Pour the broth over the couscous, meat, and vegetables; serve any remaining broth on the side as a sauce.

## CORNES DE GAZELLES
(Almond Gazelle Horns)

*1 2/3 cups all-purpose flour, sifted*
*2 cups powdered sugar*
*3 tablespoons corn oil*
*1 cup warm water*
*1 1/2 cups ground almonds*
*2 tablespoons cinnamon*
*1/4 cup orange blossom water (available in specialty food shops)*
*1 cup unsalted butter, melted*

1) Preheat oven to 350.

2) Thoroughly combine the flour and 1 cup of the powdered sugar. Add the corn oil and warm water. Form a ball with the dough and cover it with a damp cloth. Refrigerate it until ready to make the pastries.

3) To make the filling, combine the ground almonds, remaining powdered sugar, cinnamon, butter, and orange blossom water. It should be about the consistency of marzipan.

4) Divide the dough into thirds. Roll out one piece of the dough paper-thin, and cut it into strips 3 inches long and 1 1/2 inches wide. Place 1 1/2 teaspoons of the almond mixture on each strip, then roll the strips diagonally into horn shapes. Repeat this procedure with the rest of the dough and filling. The recipe should yield ten pastries.

5) Bake the horns on a greased cookie sheet for 30 to 45 minutes or until the cookies are firm but not brown. These pastries are traditionally served with green or gunpowder tea flavored with fresh mint and sweetened with plenty of sugar. Sometimes the tea is seasoned with orange blossom water.

# THE EMBASSY OF THE
# FEDERAL REPUBLIC OF NIGERIA

*Dinner for Six*

## AKARA
*(Ground Bean Appetizer)*

## JOLLOF
*(African Chicken with Rice Casserole)*

## DODO
*(Plantain)*

## ASARO MARIA
*(Banana-Coconut Pudding)*

## BEVERAGE

## GREEN TEA

Nigeria, on the west coast of Africa, just below the Sahara Desert, is a sunny, warm country, and home to sixty million people. Formerly a British colony, it has been independent since 1960. Lagos, its beautiful capital, boasts wide, gleaming beaches washed by the Atlantic Ocean. It is a country rich in fruits, vegetables, flowers, cocoa, peanuts, petroleum, iron, and bauxite. Nigeria's many tourist attractions include the world-famous game reserves of Yankari and Borgu.

There have been numerous changes in the Nigerian government in recent years. The present government is headed by a military leader, Major General Ghadamosi Babanginda.

The current Nigerian Ambassador to the United States, who has held the post now for two years, is Ignatius Olisemeka. Prior to that he represented his country in Spain and in the Vatican. Schooled in Nigeria and at the London School of Economics, Ambassador Olisemeka is a respected and popular figure in Washington. He and his wife, Madame Gloria Olisemeka, enjoy entertaining at their residence, a lovely sprawling country house in Chevy Chase, one of Washington's most elegant suburbs.

French chef Simeon Brisseau prepares the embassy dinners, in the ambassador's residence. The house is filled with Nigerian wood carvings and art pieces. Ivory carvings and polished ebony sculptures, especially of tall curvaceous women, grandly represent Nigeria as a center of African culture.

The menus and recipes included here use fruits and vegetables indigenous to Nigeria–bananas, plantains, rice, tomatoes, and red peppers–and they are the key ingredients in this traditional Nigerian meal. The menu represents the best recipes of the four tribes that make up Nigeria. Although alcohol was never served in the past, white wine is now included with the appetizer and main course. During the toast, which is "Cheers," a splash of wine is spilled as a loving libation to the spirits of the guests' ancestors.

## FEDERAL REPUBLIC OF NIGERIA

## AKARA
(Ground Bean Appetizer)

2 1/2 cups dry pinto or black beans
salt to taste
1/2 tablespoon freshly-ground pepper
1 medium onion, finely chopped
1 cup water
3 eggs, beaten lightly
2 cups vegetable oil

1) Soak the beans for an hour in warm water to cover. Remove the skins that come off or become loose. Grind or process the bean pulp into a smooth paste, adding a little water if necessary.

2) Put the ground beans into a bowl and add the salt, pepper, and onion. Add the cup of water to the mix. Next add the beaten eggs and mix thoroughly. When the mixture is the right consistency–dough-like and easily molded–shape it into round patties, about 1 1/2 inches in diameter and 1/4 inch thick. It should make 12.

3) Heat all the oil in a 10-inch skillet and fry the patties in three batches of four each. They should be cooked over medium heat until golden brown–about 2 minutes. Akara is a finger food and should be served warm.

FEDERAL REPUBLIC OF NIGERIA

## JOLLOF
### (African Chicken with Rice Casserole)

2 pounds chicken, cut up
salt and pepper to taste
4 cups water
3 medium onions
1 cup vegetable oil
6 medium size tomatoes, sliced
3 large red peppers, sliced, seeds removed
1 cup tomato paste
3 cups water
1 cup rice
1/2 teaspoon salt

1) Season the chicken pieces with salt and pepper; cover and let stand for 15 minutes.

2) Bring the 4 cups of water to a boil in a 5-quart Dutch oven. Put the chicken in and cook until tender—about 30 minutes. Remove the chicken from the broth and pat each piece dry. Reserve the cooking broth.

3) Chop one of the onions coarsely; quarter the other two.

4) Heat the oil in a deep, 14-inch skillet until a piece of the chopped onion sizzles actively when dropped into the oil. Add the rest of the chopped onion to the oil, and then the chicken. Fry until the chicken is golden brown and crisp. Remove the chicken; reserve the oil and onions.

5) Put one of the quartered onions, half the tomato slices, and half the pepper slices in a blender and chop at low speed. Empty the blender and repeat this with the other onion and the rest of the tomatoes and peppers. Add this chopped mixture to the reserved oil and onions in which the chicken has been fried. Cook for 15 minutes over medium heat.

6) Finally, add the tomato paste, and then stir in the reserved chicken broth a little at a time. Cook for an additional 15 minutes over low heat.

7) During this last step, cook the rice. Bring the water to a boil and stir in the rice and salt. Cover the pot, turn the heat to low, and simmer for 15 minutes. Then uncover the pot and let the rice stand until it is dry and fluffy. Toss it with a fork.

8) To serve, place the chicken in the center of a large platter and surround it with the rice. Then top the chicken and rice with the vegetable mixture. Serve with any dry, white wine.

## DODO
(Plantain)

*9 green or yellow plantains (available at Hispanic grocery stores)*
*salt to taste*
*4 cups palm oil, or vegetable oil as a substitute*

1) Remove the skins of the plantains by cutting through them lengthwise and opening them with your fingers. Cut the plantains into 1/4-inch slices, cutting diagonally to form ovals about twice as long as they are wide. Salt them to taste.

2) Heat 1/4 inch of the oil in a 10-inch skillet over medium heat. Fry the plantain slices, a few at a time, until brown--about 5 minutes. Add oil as necessary to maintain a depth of 1/4 inch. Serve the plaintain hot, with Jollof.

## ASARO MARIA
(Banana-Coconut Pudding)

*2 small coconuts*
*4 eggs*
*2 tablespoons sugar*
*2 cups coconut milk*
*4 large ripe bananas*
*1 teaspoon butter*

1)  Preheat the oven to 350.

2)  Pierce the eyes of the coconuts with an awl and pour out the milk.   (If necessary, this may be supplemented with canned coconut milk to make 2 cups.)  Pry the coconut meat loose from the shells, break it into small pieces, and grate it in a blender.

3)  Beat the eggs and add the sugar and the coconut milk, mixing well.   Then add the grated coconut and mix all of them thoroughly.

4)  Peel the bananas and mash them with a fork.  Add them to the coconut mixture.  Grease a 9-inch pie plate with the butter and pour the pudding mixture into it.  Bake 15 minutes, or until golden brown. Serve warm or cold.

# EMBASSY OF THE
# POLISH PEOPLE'S REPUBLIC

*Serves Six*

## BARSZCZ USZKA
*(Beet Borscht)*

## PSTRAG W MIGDALACH
*(Trout)*

## ZRAZY PO POLSKU
*(Rolled Beef Steaks)*

## FIOLETOWA KAPUSTA
*(Red Cabbage)*

## KOMPOT
*(Fruit Compote)*

## FAWORKI
*(Fried Cookies)*

## VODKA

"We give our hearts to our guests before we share food together."  This was the greeting from Madame Zofia Ludwiczak, wife of Poland's chief representative to the United States, Charge d'Affaires Zdzislaw Ludwiczak.

Madame Ludwiczak's welcome reflected the warm hospitality characteristic of the Polish people, whether in their native land or in another country.  The luncheon to which we were invited, and for which the menu and recipes are included here, was served in the dining room of the embassy next to the main drawing room.  It is a formal room, elegantly decorated in white and antique gold, with a magnificent collection of Polish silver.  The table decorations were beautifully-arranged vases of red and white flowers (these are Poland's national colors), gold-rimmed white china, and crystal glassware, all set on a glistening white tablecloth.

Polish dinners and receptions are well attended.  The embassy is a large gray stone mansion, built in 1909, on Washington's 16th Street.  From the formal marble entrance hall, a wide staircase leads to a spacious reception room and a blue and white drawing room.  The centerpiece here is an enormous black grand piano belonging to Ignacy Jan Paderewski, one of the world's greatest pianists and composers, who also served as the first Polish prime minister after World War I.  The piano was specially built to fit Paderewski's small hands.  Above it hangs a portrait of him.

The Polish people love eating and partying.  Two Polish Embassy cooks, with the assistance of the skilled diplomatic wives, love to entertain and serve their traditional Polish dishes.  The grandest party is on the occasion of the Polish National Holiday, July 22.  Christmas is also a very big occasion.

Polish cuisine evolved over the centuries and has a character all its own, despite the influences of bordering Czechoslovakia, Germany, and the Soviet Union.  One can also taste Turkish and Arabic influences, as well as those of France and Italy.  But even with all the contributions from other cultures, Poland's cuisine reflects her people's own unique style and flavor.

No discussion of Poland's tables would be complete without mentioning the traditional drinks. One is *miod*, an alcoholic beverage made from honey and mixed with spices. Sweet and no stronger than wine, it has been drunk in Poland for centuries by kings and peasants alike. It can be drunk cold or hot, and is often used for warming up after a winter's hunt.

Polish vodkas–Wyborowa, Zubrowka, and Zytnia Vodka–are held by many to be the best in the world. Vodka is best served straight and very cold; iced but not on the rocks. It is served before a dinner and also during the meal.

So, with the menu and recipes provided by the Embassy of Poland, Charge d'Affaires and Madame Ludwiczak, raise a glass to your friends with the Polish toast: "Na Zdrovie!"..."To Your Health."

## BARSZCZ USZKA
(Beet Borscht)

2 pounds fresh beets
6 cups water
2 stalks celery, cut in 4- or 5-inch lengths
4 dry mushrooms, soaked overnight and chopped into 1/4 inch
   pieces
3 medium onions
4 tablespoons red wine vinegar
3 tablespooons sugar
salt and pepper, to taste
1 tablespoon butter
USZKA (ravioli stuffed with mushrooms, see following page)

1) Cut the beets into large pieces and place in the water. Add the celery and mushrooms and bring to a boil.

2) Peel two of the onions and smoke over an open flame. (Stick a fork into the center and hold over the fire until the onions turn a little black.) Add them to the soup.

3) Season the soup with the vinegar, sugar, salt, and pepper. Bring it back to a boil and cook for one hour over low heat.

4) Chop the remaining onion and saute it in the butter over moderate heat. When it is slightly pink and transparent, add it to the soup mixture.

5) Let the soup set overnight to develop the flavor fully. When ready to serve it, pour it through a strainer, discard the vegetables, and serve the clear broth very hot. Add a few USZKA (see following page) to each serving.

### USZKA

3 cups flour
4 large dry mushrooms, soaked overnight and chopped into 1/4-
   inch pieces
1 tablespoon butter
4 chicken bouillon cubes, crumbled
1 medium onion, finely chopped
salt and pepper to taste
2-3 tablespoons oil

1) To prepare the dough, sift the flour into a medium-size bowl and gradually add cold water, mixing the dough with one hand and pouring water with the other. Add as much water as needed to make a soft dough. Knead it until smooth and elastic.

2) Roll out small pieces of the dough on a well-floured surface. The dough should be just thick enough to hold together when stuffed. Cut circles of the dough with a glass 1 1/2-inches in diameter.

3) To prepare the stuffing, fry the mushrooms and onions in the butter for 7 minutes. Add the chicken bouillon cubes during the frying. Season with salt and pepper to taste.

4) Put the stuffing mixture into a blender and mix it at medium speed until it is the consistency of ground meat.

5) Place about 1/3 teaspoon of the stuffing onto each circle of dough; fold them into semicircles and press the edges firmly together. Boil a few of them at a time in salted water until they rise to the surface. The time for this will vary.

6) Remove the uszka from the water and set aside until ready to serve with the borscht. Immediately before serving, heat the oil in a 12-inch skillet and fry the uszka over medium heat until slightly crisp.

## PSTRAG W MIGDALACH
### (Trout)

3 medium-size trout, skinned and cut into 6 filets
salt to taste
2 eggs, beaten
4 tablespoons bread crumbs
1/2 cup fresh slivered almonds
3 tablespoons butter

1) Salt the fish filets if desired. Coat each piece with the egg, then sprinkle both sides with the bread crumbs and almonds.

2) Fry the filets in the butter, turning once, until both sides are brown about 5 minutes over medium heat. Serve immediately with French bread and butter.

## ZRAZY PO POLSKU
### (Rolled Beef Steaks)

2 pounds round rib roast
4 tablespoons brown mustard
salt and pepper to taste
3 medium onions, finely chopped
1 pound fresh mushrooms, chopped
6-8 tablespoons oil
l pound thick-sliced bacon
1-2 cups water
2 beef bouillon cubes
3 tablespoons flour
1/2 cup sour cream
KASZA (buckwheat groats, see following page)

1) Rinse the meat and remove any fat or membrane. Slice it across the grain making flat steaks about 1/4-inch thick. Pound the steaks with a dampened meat hammer to a thickness of 1/8-inch.

2) Spread each steak with a thin layer of mustard, then salt and pepper to taste.

3) Fry the onions and mushrooms together in 3 tablespoons of the oil. Add salt and pepper to taste.

4) Lay a strip of bacon across each steak; trim ends if necessary. Put about a teaspoon of the onion/mushroom mixture on each steak and spread it out evenly. Reserve the rest.

5) Roll the steaks around their stuffings and tie them with string, or secure them with toothpicks.

6) Heat the remaining oil in a 12-inch skillet and brown the steak rolls on both sides over medium heat.

7) Place the rolls in a saucepan large enough to have no more than two layers. Dissolve the bouillon cubes in a cup of water and add it to the pan. If the meat is not covered, add a little more water. Add the remaining mushroom/onion mixture. Stew the rolls over low heat, covered, for about an hour.

8) After the rolls have cooked, mix the flour with enough water to make it the consistency of heavy cream, and then stir in the sour cream. Put this liquid into the saucepan to make a gravy. Add salt if desired.

9) Serve two steak rolls to each diner, and accompany them with KASZA (see following page).

### KASZA
(Buckwheat Groats)

*2 cups whole buckwheat groats*
*2 tablespoons butter*
*salt to taste*
*4 cups water*

1) In a 10 by 10 by 4-inch flameproof and ovenproof pan, fry the buckwheat in the butter for about 2 minutes. Add the water and cook over medium heat until all the liquid is absorbed–15 to 25 minutes.

2) Preheat the oven to 150.

3) Cover the pan and bake the buckwheat for 30 minutes. Serve with the meat and gravy.

### FIOLETOWA KAPUSTA
(Red Cabbage)

*1 small head red cabbage*
*1 teaspoon salt*
*5 tablespoons lemon juice*
*2 tablespoons sugar*
*1 large onion, finely chopped*
*2 medium apples, finely chopped*
*5 tablespoons oil*

1) Shred the cabbage and boil it for 8 to 10 minutes in salted water to cover. Drain and let cool.

2) Add the lemon juice, sugar, onions, apples, and oil. Mix well and refrigerate before serving.

### KOMPOT
(Fruit Compote)

*1 apple, peeled and cored*
*2 pears, peeled and cored*
*1/4 pound fresh cherries, pitted*
*6 plums, peeled and pitted*
*2 slices lemon*
*1 clove*
*3/4 cup sugar, or to taste*
*4 cups water*

1) Put the fruit, the clove, and the sugar in the water and boil for 30 minutes.

2) Remove the lemon slices and refrigerate the compote. Serve cold.

## FAWORKI
### (Fried Cookies)

*4 egg yolks, lightly beaten*
*1 teaspoon sugar*
*1 teaspoon butter, softened*
*2 drops vanilla*
*1/2 cup warm water*
*10 ounces white all-purpose flour*
*oil (enough to fill a 10-inch skillet to a depth of 1-inch)*
*1/2 cup confectioners sugar*

1) Put the egg yolks, sugar, butter, vanilla, and warm water in a mixing bowl. Gradually add the flour, mixing until the dough is soft but not sticky. Knead the dough for 5 minutes, then hit it several times with a rolling pin.

2) Cut the dough into six equal parts and put them in a plastic bag for about 20 minutes.

3) Take one piece of dough out at a time, and roll it into a very thin sheet on a well-floured surface. Cut the sheet into rectangles about 4 1/2-inch long and 1 1/2-inch wide. Cut a 2-inch slit lengthwise down the center of each one.

4) Pick up one end of each strip and insert it through the slot in the middle, then take one end in each hand and pull in opposite directions. Stretch the dough firmly but not to the breaking point. The result will resemble a bow tie with a sort of diamond-shaped hole in the middle.

5) Repeat the above process with the remaining pieces of dough. Keeping them enclosed in the plastic bag in the meantime will prevent them from drying out.

6) When all the cookies are made, heat the oil over medium heat until a test strip of the dough bubbles actively. Put no more than 8 cookies in the oil at a time and leave them for no more than 30 to 40 seconds, turning them once.

7) Drain the fried cookies on absorbent paper to remove excess oil, and let them cool slightly.

8) Put the powdered sugar into a plastic bag and add the cookies, a few at a time. Shake gently to coat and place them on a serving tray. This recipe yields approximately 60 cookies.

9) These are very pretty and tasty served with strong black coffee at the end of the meal.

# THE EMBASSY OF PORTUGAL

*Dinner for Eight*

## PURE DE BATATA E CEBOULA COM COENTROS
*(Potato and Onion Puree with Fresh Coriander)*

## BACALHAU DOURADO
*(Golden Codfish with Green Salad)*

## LOMBO DE PORCO ASSADO DE VINHO E ALHOS
*(Roasted Pork Loin Marinated in White Wine and Herbs)*

## SOBREMESA
*(Custard With Burnt Sugar)*

## WINES

Algarve White
Red Colares
Madeira
LBV Vintage Port

Portugal, on the Atlantic Ocean, was occupied by the Phoenicians, the Greeks, the Romans, the Visigoths, and the Moors, until it finally emerged as a nation in the twelveth century, under the rule of King Afonso Henrique. From then on Portugal became the center of the world's greatest navigators. Henry the Navigator was a Portugese prince who established one of the world's most famous navigation schools.

The Portuguese sailed to China where they discovered tea. They introduced it to England, where the English named it "tea" from the Chinese TCHA, marked with a simple "T" on the bales. It was the Portuguese who bought the printing press to Japan, wine and garlic to India, and spices from the Orient and Africa to all of Europe. Portugal is an ancient country with a cosmopolitan outlook and its food reflects a dozen cultures.

The dining room at the Portuguese Embassy is a connoisseur's blue and white dream. The walls are tiled with the world-famous blue and white tiles from the eighteenth century. They surround a white porcelain fountain topped with a gold framed portrait of Queen Mary. The tables and chairs are hand-carved seventeenth century oak wood from Portugal.

Dining in this elegant room includes lots of spirited conversation. Every Portuguese has a famous navigator in his family, and the conversation touches on those early voyages to Japan, Ghana, Ethiopia, the Americas, India and the Persian Gulf, and the languages include Russian, Hindi, Arabic, Chinese and English.

The Portugese say: "We look at the sea as an extension of our country." And so fish, caught fresh every day, is a mainstay of their dining, along with potatoes, olive oil, pork with herbs and wine cabbage, codfish, partridge, and rich soups.

The Portuguese excel in sweets, recipes for which were put together in the ancient convents and monestaries. As a result these luscious deserts have such names as: Angel's Breast,

Nun's Bellies, Heavenly Cakes and Angel Food.

The dinners at the imposing cream colored, stone and brick embassy are supervised by the ambassador's wife, Isabel Bandeira de Mello Mathias. The recipes included here are embassy favorites.

Ambassador Leonardo and Madame Mathias, have covered the globe as diplomats. He has served in Capetown, Spain, Italy, Iraq, Geneva, and at the Unted Nations in New York. The ambassador has a brilliant political mind, and helped negotiate Portugal's accession to the Common Market which the embassy describes as "the fulfillment of Portugal's destiny in Europe's mainstream."

Although the ancient Phoenicians are credited with introducing wine to Portugal, today it is the world's seventh producer of fine wine.

So, enjoy this very special Portuguese dinner and join in the Portuguese toast: "Asua Saude" ... "To Your Health and Well Being."

## PURE DE BATATA E CEBOULA COM COENTROS
### (Potato and Onion Puree with Fresh Coriander)

*10 cups water*
*1 pound red potatoes, peeled and quartered*
*1 five-ounce onion, peeled and quartered*
*2 tablespoons plus 1 teaspoon olive oil*
*1 tablespoon salt (or to taste)*
*1/2 teaspoon white pepper*
*1 bunch fresh coriander*

1) In a large saucepan heat the 10 cups of water to boiling. Add the potatoes, onions, olive oil, salt, and pepper. Boil for 15 minutes over medium heat or until potatoes are flaky.

2) Wash the coriander thoroughly in cold running water; chop into 3-inch pieces.

3) Remove the pan from the heat and add the coriander stems; mix well. Puree the mixture in a blender or a food processor, in small batches if necessary. Return it to the pan and check for seasoning.

4) If the soup is thicker than cream, add water until the desired thickness is achieved. Serve at once or keep, refrigerated, up to 2 days; when ready to serve, bring to the boil, add 2 tablespoons finely chopped coriander, simmer for 1 1/2 minutes, and serve.

## BACALHAU DOURADO
### (Golden Codfish)

*2 pounds salt cod*
*1 pound french-fried shoestring potatoes (pre-cut frozen are*
*recommended)*
*1 1/4 cups finely chopped onion*
*1 cup plus 2 teaspoons olive oil, or more if needed*
*8 eggs*
*1 teaspoon freshly ground black pepper*
*4 tablespoons finely chopped parsley*
*1 can small black pitted olives, coarsely chopped preferably*
*Portuguese*

1) Prepare the salt cod according to the instructions given under The Federative Republic of Brazil, on page 4 .

2) Put the cod in a large kettle and cover with as much water as the kettle allows. Bring to a boil, uncover, reduce heat to moderate, and simmer for 20 minutes or until the fish flakes easily. Drain and let cool.

3) Prepare the potatoes according to the package instructions. Keep warm in a 250-degree oven.

4) With a small knife, remove the skin and bones from the cod, watching for small bones. Flake the fish coarsely.

5) Divide all the ingredients into two batches, each to be cooked in a twelve-inch skillet, one skillet is not large enough.

6) Heat 1/2 cup of olive oil over moderate heat until a blue haze forms. Add half the onions, and cook for about 5 minutes until light golden brown, stirring with a wooden spoon.

7) Add half the cod and cook for a few minutes, until some of the oil is absorbed. Add more oil if needed.

8) Beat four eggs and half the pepper until frothy, then pour into the pan with the cod and onions. Add another teaspoon of olive oil; the chef says, "Remember--olive oil and codfish is a marriage made in heaven." Cook over low heat, stirring with a spatula to mix thoroughly. When the eggs are barely set but not hard, fold in the warm potatoes.

9) Transfer to a heated platter, sprinkle with half of the parsley, and garnish with half of the olives.

10) Repeat steps 6 through 9 with the remaining ingredients.

## GREEN SALAD

*2 heads Boston or Bibb lettuce*
*2 bunches watercress*
*1/3 cup olive oil*
*2 tablespoons wine vinegar*
*1/4 teaspoon salt*
*1/4 teaspoon dry mustard*
*1/8 teaspoon freshly-ground black pepper*

1) Mix enough of the lettuce and watercress to make 8 cups of greens. Refrigerate for at least an hour before serving.

2) Mix the remaining ingredients and refrigerate for an hour. When ready to serve, shake vigorously, pour over the greens, and toss well.

### LOMBO DE PORCO ASSADO DE VINHO E ALHOS
(Roasted Pork Loin Marinated in White Wine and Herbs)

*2 cups dry white wine*
*1/4 cup wine vinegar*
*4 large garlic cloves, finely chopped*
*2 medium bay leaves, crumbled*
*1 teaspoon marjoram, crumbled*
*1 teaspoon savory, crumbled*
*1 tablespoon plus 1 teaspoon salt (or to taste)*
*1 1/2 teaspoons black pepper (or to taste)*
*1 five-pound pork loin*
*4 large carrots, cut into 3-inch sticks, then quartered lengthwise*
*40 small spring potatoes, one inch or less in diameter*
*24 stalks fresh asparagus*
*Thin orange slices for garnish*

1) To prepare the marinade, combine 1 1/2 cups of the wine with the vinegar, garlic, bay leaves, marjoram, savory, salt, and pepper. Stir until well blended, making sure the salt in dissolved.

2) With your hands, rub the marinade into the pork loin, distributing the garlic and herbs evenly. Refrigerate overnight.

3) Preheat the oven to 375. Pour about an inch of water into a roasting pan and place the loin on a rack above it, fat side up. If there is marinade left, pour it onto the meat.

4) Roast, uncovered, for an hour or longer, until the roast is slightly brown. Mix the remaining 1/2 cup of wine with 1/2 cup of water and sprinkle a little of this liquid onto the roast.

5) Continue roasting at 375 for another hour, sprinkling the meat occasionally with the wine and water. Add water to the pan if it is dry. At the end of the 2 hours, test the roast with a fork. If it is not tender, turn the oven down to 250 and continue roasting, checking for tenderness every 20 minutes.

6) While the roast is cooking, boil the carrots and potatoes until they are almost done, about 12 to 15 minutes. Add them to the roasting pan for the last half hour. At this time you may also move the roast off the rack into the broth in the pan.

7) Just before serving the roast, prepare the asparagus. Break off the tough ends and discard. Wash the stalks carefully to remove sand, then lay them flat in a pan and add water to cover. Cook until tender, about 15 to 20 minutes. Drain, place in a warm dish, and spread with butter.

8) When the roast is done, transfer it to a heated platter, surround it with the carrots and potatoes, and garnish it with orange slices if desired. Serve the asparagus separately.

## SOBREMESA
### (Custard With Burnt Sugar)

*4 cups heavy cream*
*1 vanilla bean*
*pinch of salt*
*8 egg yolks*
*3/4 cup plus 2 tablespoons white sugar*
*8 tablespoons light brown sugar*

1) Preheat oven to 300.

2) In a heavy saucepan, combine the cream, vanilla bean, and salt. Cook over medium heat until the mixture begins to simmer, about five minutes. Set aside.

3) In a large bowl, combine the egg yolks and the white sugar. Stir with a wooden spoon until thoroughly mixed.

4) Remove the vanilla bean from the cream. (It may be reserved for use on another occasion.) Carefully pour the hot cream over the yolks and sugar and stir gently. Strain this mixture into a container with a pouring spout. Skim the bubbles off the surface.

5) Place eight 3/4-cup ramekins in a roasting pan and fill them to the rims with custard. Fill the pan with water to half the height of the ramekins. Cover loosely with aluminum foil and bake for 1 hour and 15 minutes, or until the custard is firm around the edges. The centers will become firm when chilled.

6) Remove the ramekins from the water and let cool. Cover and refrigerate for at least 3 hours, or up to 2 days. If pools of liquid appear on the surface, blot with a paper towel before proceeding.

# PORTUGAL

7)  Preheat the broiler.

8)  Place the ramekins on a baking sheet, then distribute 1 tablespoon of brown sugar evenly on each.  Place in the broiler close to the heat source, and broil until the sugar is caramelized.  Watch closely, checking every 30 seconds.  Do not keep under the broiler for more than 2 minutes.

9)  Remove the custard from the broiler.  It may be served hot, at room temperature, or chilled (up to 3 1/2 hours).

# THE EMBASSY OF THE
# UNION OF SOVIET SOCIALIST REPUBLICS

*Dinner for Six*

## OEUFS A LA RUSSE ET VODKA
*(Hard Boiled Eggs with Caviar served with Vodka)*

## OUKHA A LA SOUZDALJENNE
*(Fish Soup from South Alienne)*

## ESCALOPES DE VEAU AMANDINE
*(Veal Scallops with Almonds)*

## LEGUMES
*(Vegetables)*

## FRUIT COMPOTE

## BEVERAGES

## VODKA
## WINES

# UNION OF SOVIET SOCIALIST REPUBLICS

The Embassy of the Union of Soviet Socialist Republics is the home of His Excellency Ambassador Yuri Dubinin and Madame Dubinin who arrived in the United States in May 1986. They represent the world's largest country. When the sun is setting on Moscow, it is rising over Vladivostock in the East. This huge country crosses eleven time zones, borders twelve countries and three oceans. Extending from the Arctic to the Black Sea, and east to the Pacific, the Union of the Soviet Socialist Republics is a nation of 104 officially recognized ethnic groups, with a population of 277,465,000 people.

The embassy building, occupied by Soviet ambassadors since 1933, is a historic mansion on 16th Street just a few blocks from the White House. It is the scene of lavish parties and receptions, celebrating such events as the visiting Bolshoi Ballet, Moyseyev Dancers, opera stars, writers, and artists. The Soviets love a good party and the embassy, with its red carpets, brilliant chandeliers and massive gold-framed paintings, is the perfect setting for these lavish receptions and dinners.

Russian cuisine is replete with exotic and exciting contrasts because of the unusual variety of climates, landscapes, soils, peoples, customs, and foods in the country. European Russia alone is a mosaic of peoples composed of Estonians, Latvians and Lithuanians on the Baltic; Armenians, Azerbaidjanis and Georgians in the Southern Caucusus; and Slavs in the Russian Federation, the Ukraine and Byelorussia. Each of these nationalities has its own proud traditions in culture, cooking and language.

Russian cookery has had a tempestuous past, being derived from nomadic Asian tribes, Slavs, Vikings, Turks and Tartars. The Slavs and Vikings served a convivial pre-meal spread of game, meats and freshly caught fish. This was the origination of the modern *zakusky*, meaning "bite down," a delicious buffet served before the main meal and washed down with ice cold vodka.

French and German recipes were introduced to Russia in the

seventeenth century by Peter the Great who imported French chefs and even took over the royal kitchens himself to prepare special meals. A lover of good food, Peter's favorites were Dutch cheeses, German sausages, and roast goose, as well as French sauces and cream soups.

The greatest gourmet among Russian rulers was Czar Alexander I who continued the French culinary craze when he hired the world-famous French chef Antonin Careme to supervise the imperial kitchens. For the Czar, Careme created the famous dessert, Charlotte Russe.

Today, the Soviet Union does not feature the wildly lavish entertaining of the Imperial Court. But the history and cooking traditions of the U.S.S.R.'s sixteen Republics have made Russian cuisine one of the most varied and interesting in the world. The menu presented here was sent directly from the Kremlin to the Soviet Embassy here in Washinton, D.C.

Entertaining throughout the Soviet Union is epitomized by spirited dining, and no party would be complete without vodka. Vodka, literally translated as "little water" and now known as the Russian national drink, is served ice cold in small cups. You might try serving a flavored vodka, as they do in Russia; pepper, herb, cherry or lemon. The toast raised before and during every dinner is a hearty "Mir i Druzhba!" . . . "Peace and Friendship!"

UNION OF SOVIET SOCIALIST REPUBLICS

## OEUFS A LA RUSSE ET VODKA
### (Hard Boiled Eggs with Caviar served with Vodka)

*6 hardboiled eggs, chilled and cut in half lengthwise*
*1 cup sour cream*
*1/2 cup black caviar*
*2 tablespoons lemon juice*
*freshly ground pepper to taste*

1) Mix a sauce of the sour cream, black caviar, lemon juice, and ground pepper. Chill

2) Place two egg halves on each of six plates, yolk side down.

3) Cover with the chilled sauce and serve with cold vodka.

Note: Caviar, from the Turkish word "khavyah," called "ikra" in the Soviet Union, is the carefully extracted roe of four species of sturgeon. Caviar connoisseurs insist that the finest caviar, the "black gold," should be spooned and eaten directly from the ice-packed container. Some, however, prefer to serve caviar on toast with lemon juice, chopped hard cooked eggs and chopped onion on the side.

## OUKHA A LA SOUZDALJENNE
(Fish Soup from South Alienne)

*2 lbs filet of white fish cut into bite-size pieces*
*3 medium onions, finely chopped*
*6 peppercorns*
*1 sprig parsley*
*1/8 teaspoon ground cloves*
*2 tablespoons butter*
*2 medium tomatos, peeled and chopped*
*10 pitted black olives*
*1 cucumber, peeled and chopped*
*4 tablespoons drained capers*
*1 teaspoon dill*
*6 thin slices of lemon*
*salt and freshly ground pepper to taste*

1)  Put 2 quarts of water in a heavy pot.  Add the fish trimmings (including the head and bones), one chopped onion, the peppercorns, the cloves and freshly ground pepper.  Cook over medium heat for 30 minutes.

2)  Strain and save the broth; discard the ingredients.

3)  Saute the rest of the chopped onions in butter until transluscent.  Add the tomatoes.  Stir and cook for 2 minutes.

4)  Add this mixture plus the cucumber, capers, olives, and bit-sized pieces of fish to the strained broth.

5)  Cover and cook slowly for about 10 minutes or until fish is tender.  Salt to taste.

6)  Serve in bowls garnished with lemon slices and dill.

### ESCALOPES DE VEAU AMANDINE
(Veal Scallops with Almonds)

*12 veal tenderloin scallops, 3 ounces each*
*1 cup flour*
*6 1/2 tablespoons butter*
*3/4 teaspoon red paprika*
*3 medium onions, finely chopped*
*2/3 cup ground or finely chopped almonds*
*1 cup beef broth*
*1 cup dry white wine*
*salt and pepper to taste*

1) Pound each of the veal scallops until thin, about 1/4-inch. Season with salt and pepper to taste and flour them lightly. Saute in 3 tablespoons hot butter until lightly browned. Set aside.

2) In a large, heavy skillet melt the rest of the butter over medium heat. Saute onions until golden brown. Remove pan from heat and add almonds, paprika and salt to taste. Mix until welll blended and divide into 12 portions.

3) Place veal scallops on a large flat surface. Spread the almond mixture evenly over the top surface of each scallop. Roll each scallop tightly and pin with a toothpick or tie with string.

4) Pour off most of the fat from the large heavy pan. Add the dry white wine and boil lightly for five minutes, stirring and scraping any brown bits that cling to the pan. Add the cup of beef broth and reduce heat to simmer. Return the veal rolls to the pan, cover, and simmer for 20 minutes, or until tender, turning the rolls after 10 minutes.

5) After removing the toothpicks, place the scallops on a warm platter for serving. Sprinkle with the cooking juices. Served with small potatoes that have boiled until nearly tender, then sliced and sauteed in butter until golden brown.

## LEGUMES
### (Vegetables)

1 lb. fresh green beans, trimmed and cut in half crosswise
1 medium green pepper, seeded and chopped fine
1 medium onion, minced
4 tablespoons butter
2 large tomatoes, peeled, seeded and chopped
1 tablespoon chopped fresh basil
salt and freshly ground black pepper to taste
1/2 cup sour cream

1) Boil the beans in lightly salted water for about 7 minutes. Drain and set asisde.

2) Melt butter in a heavy 10 inch pan. Add onion and green pepper and cook until soft but not browned.

3) Add the beans, tomatoes and basil and cook about 4 minutes, stirring constantly.

4) Beat salt and pepper into the sour cream and stir into the vegetables thoroughly. Taste for seasoning. Serve immediately.

### FRUIT COMPOTE

*2 lbs. fresh fruit (Peaches, pears, berries, apples, figs, oranges.)*
*2 cups sugar*
*1 tablespoon lemon juice, wine, rum or brandy*
*1 cinnamon stick*
*1 pint whipping cream, whipped and sweetened to taste*

1) Wash, peel, core, remove pits and skins from fruit.

2) Cut into halves or quarters.

3) Combine fruit, sugar, lemon juice, wine, rum or brandy, and cinnamon stick in a saucepan. Add water to cover and cook slowly until fruit is tender but not mushy.

4) Remove from heat. Discard cinnamon stick. Cool.

5) Serve cold in dessert dishes and cover with whipped cream.

## THE EMBASSY OF SPAIN

*Dinner for Six*

### PAELLA VALENCIANA
*(Valencian Paella)*

### TERNERA MECHADA COSTA DEL SOL
*(Stuffed Veal Roast with Wine Sauce)*

### LEGUMBRES SALTEADAS
*(Fresh Vegetable Saute)*

### CREMA CATALANA
*(Catalan Cream Caramel)*

### WINES

MONOPOL 1972
MARQUES DE RISCAL 1952

Spain is castanets, castles, and flamenco, beautiful beaches, and the air of a perpetual Spanish fiesta. All the beauty, sound, and color is reflected in Spanish food.

The Iberian Peninsula is located under the fortunate sign of the olive. Phoenicians planted olive groves and grape vines throughout the area, with the result that wine for drinking and olive oil for cooking are the basis for some of the finest taste thrills in the world.

The menu supplied here through the courtesy of Spanish Ambassador H.E. Gabriel Manueco and his wife, Maria Teresa Pfeiffer, includes delicious Spanish dishes that would delight the heart of any visiting royalty, including King Juan Carlos of Spain himself.

Ambassador and Madame Manueco entertain frequently and lavishly in the elegant Spanish Embassy, a white stone mansion built by a Mrs. John B. Henderson and offered to the U. S. government for the official residence of the vice president. However, Congress refused to allocate funds for it, and the property was sold to the Spanish Government in 1928. Spanish touches have since transformed the interior into a palace.

A typical Spanish patio is constructed with tiles from Seville and Valencia, and wrought-iron doors and grills from Toledo. An exotic ballroom and dining room contain a priceless collection of paintings from the Prado Museum. In the drawing room is a painting attributed to Goya; a portrait of the famous actress La Tirana. There is also original artwork by Eugenio Lucas, a follower of Goya. Crystal chandeliers from La Granja, a mosaic of Our Lady of Los Reyes, and two seventeenth-century Flemish tapestries complete the air of opulence and artistry.

Ambassador and Madame Manueco receive their guests at the entrance to the drawing room, where they offer cocktails and a variety of sherries. The sherry is served in long-stemmed glasses, especially blown in a tall, narrow shape to preserve the heady aroma of the drink.

At the appointed hour, the doors open to the adjoining dining room, where the guests find their place cards around a long oval table which accommodates twenty-four to twenty-six. For larger functions, dinner is served on the Seville Patio, where round tables encircle a center fountain bedecked with flowers.

After the meal and dessert, guests may be treated to a concert by the guitarist Andres Segovia, who often visits, or to a performance by whirling, clicking flamenco dancers. In this candlelit setting with the elegant Spanish food and wine, the favorite toast is, "Salud, Pesetas, y Amor"..."Health, Money, and Love."

## PAELLA VALENCIANA
### (Valencian Paella)

*12 medium-sized raw shrimp*
*6 little neck clams*
*6 mussels*
*2 pounds chicken, cut into 12 serving pieces*
*2 teaspoons salt*
*freshly ground black pepper*
*1/2 cup Spanish olive oil*
*1/2 cup lean boneless pork, cut into 1/4-inch cubes*
*1/2 cup finely chopped onions*
*1 teaspoon finely chopped garlic*
*3 red pimentos, cut into strips for garnishing*
*1 large tomato, peeled, seeded, and finely chopped*
*3 cups medium-grain rice*
*6 cups chicken broth*
*1/4 teaspoon ground saffron*
*2 cups frozen green peas, thawed*
*3 pimientos, cut into strips*
*2 lemons, each cut lengthwise into 6 wedges*

1) Shell and devein the shrimp, leaving the tails intact. Scrub the clams and mussels thoroughly with a stiff brush under cold running water. Remove the black beards from the mussels.

2) Steam the clams and mussels open in a 10-inch pan with about an inch of water. Remove the half shells which do not contain the meat and discard them. Also discard any of the shellfish which do not open or which contain sand. Set the seafood aside.

3) Pat the chicken pieces dry with a paper towel and season them with 1 teaspoon of the salt and some pepper. In a heavy 10-inch skillet or Dutch oven, heat 1/4 cup of the olive oil over high heat. Add the chicken pieces and brown them well on all sides--about 15 minutes over medium heat. Remove them as they are cooked and set them aside.

4) Discard the fat remaining in the pan and put in the rest of the olive oil. When it is hot, add the pork, browning it quickly on all sides over medium heat. Add the onion, garlic, and tomato; stir constantly. Cook until the mixture is thickened–about 30 minutes–then transfer it to a 16-inch paella pan or a large flameproof baking dish.

5) Preheat the oven to 400.

6) Add the rice to the pan and mix thoroughly, over low heat. Pour in the chicken broth. Bring it to a boil, then add the saffron and stir until the yellow color is evenly distributed. Taste the liquid for seasoning and add salt if necessary.

7) Place the chicken, shrimp, mussels, and clams on top of the paella. Sprinkle the peas over it and garnish it with the pimiento strips.

8) Place the pan in the oven for 30 minutes. Serve the paella directly from the pan, garnished with the lemon wedges. This recipe makes six main-course servings; as an appetizer, it will serve more than six.

Note: Paella is the Spanish dish best-known abroad. It is cooked all over Spain, with slight variations, but it is at its glorious best along the Valencian coast. A dry Utiel or Requena wine complements it well. Above all, olive oil is essential. Paella without it is not paella.

## TERNERA MECHADA COSTA DEL SOL
(Stuffed Veal Roast with Wine Sauce

*1 3-pound veal roast (preferably top round)*
*12 small green olives, pitted*
*6 slices bacon*
*salt and pepper*
*4 tablespoons olive oil*
*3 cups chopped onion*
*3/4 cup Sanson Vino de Malaga, or Bristol Cream Sherry*
*3 cups beef stock*

1) Preheat the oven to 500.

2) Lay the veal roast out flat. Puncture it in 12 places with a sharp skewer. Place the olives and the bacon onto the roast, and season it with salt and pepper. Roll the roast around the stuffing, and tie it with twine so it will retain its shape while cooking.

3) Place the roast in a 14-inch pan, and brush it with the olive oil. Put it into the oven, turn down the heat to 450, and roast it for 15 minutes, turning it once so it will brown evenly on both sides.

4) Add the chopped onions to the pan and roast for another 15 minutes, then add the wine and return the roast to the oven for 5 more minutes.

5) Lower the oven temperature to 350; pour the beef stock into the pan and cook for another 10 minutes.

6) Remove the veal from the oven; slice it and arrange the slices on a warm serving platter. Strain the liquids in the roasting pan and serve them separately, in a warmed gravy boat.

## LEGUMBRES SALTEADAS
### (Fresh Vegetable Saute)

2 zucchini
salt to taste
2 large carrots, peeled
2 young white turnips, peeled
2 tablespoons butter, or more as needed
1 package frozen string beans, thawed
1 package frozen peas, thawed
pepper to taste
1 tablespoon chives
1 tablespoon minced parsley

1) Wash the zucchini, cut off the ends, and slice them into 1/8-inch rounds. Toss them in a bowl with a sprinkling of salt and let them drain while preparing the other vegetables. Slice the carrots and turnips into 1/4-inch rounds. These vegetables may be prepared in advance and refrigerated.

2) Ten minutes before serving, heat the butter in a 12-inch frying pan or wok and add the carrots and turnips. Toss them continually over high heat for 5 minutes. Add the string beans and peas and continue tossing, adding more butter if needed.

4) While the first four vegetables cook, pat the zucchini dry with paper towels. Add it to the pan and cook for another 3 minutes.

5) The vegetables should be cooked only until they are lightly crunchy, and should retain their color. Toss with more butter if you wish, and add the pepper, chives, and parsley. Serve at once.


### CREMA CATALANA
(Catalan Cream Caramel)


*4 cups whole milk*
*2 sticks cinnamon*
*grated rind of 1 lemon*
*9 egg yolks*
*4 1/2 tablespoons cornstarch*
*3/4 cup sugar*


1) Heat 3 cups of the milk in a saucepan with the cinnamon sticks and the lemon rind. Bring it to a boil and simmer it for 5 minutes.

2) Add 1/2 cup of the remaining milk to the egg yolks and whisk them thoroughly until light and fluffy.

3) Blend the cornstarch with the last 1/2 cup of milk until a thick smooth paste forms.

4) Strain the hot milk into a clean pan and add a half cup of the sugar, the egg yolks, and the cornstarch paste.

5) Cook the custard over a very low flame, stirring constantly until it thickens. Pour it into a lightly-buttered Pyrex baking dish (about 10 by 10 by 4-inch) and allow it to cool.

6) When the custard is firm and set (after about 45 minutes, or when a knife inserted near the center comes out clean), sprinkle the remaining sugar over the surface, and place it under the oven broiler until the sugar turns golden brown.

## THE EMBASSY OF
## THE KINGDOM OF THAILAND

*Dinner for Six*

### LAAB NUR SARANAE
*(Spicy Beef with Mint Leaves)*

### PAW PIER
*(Spring Rolls)*

### KUNG PUD BROCCOLI
*(Fried Broccoli with Shrimp)*

### KALUM PLEE
*(Cabbage Salad)*

### MALAGOH SOM TUM
*(Papaya Salad)*

### KAI YANG
*(Roasted Chicken)*

### SANG KAYA
*(Custard Dessert)*

Thailand, with its jewel-encrusted temples, Great Buddhas, majestic palaces, resplendent silks, and multicolored fruits and vegetables, is a land of extraordinary hues and exotic tastes. Today Thailand–"Land of the Free"–is ruled by American-born King Blumibol Adulyadej. He and his beautiful wife, Sirikit, are held in awe by the Thai people; their preferences can bring about an overnight change in the country's trends and customs.

Dining well has always been an important part of Thai life. In the early 1800s, King Rama II, while still a prince, wrote the Boat Songs. This was a series of beautiful poems in praise of his true love–and of her wonderful cooking. Long before <u>Anna and the King of Siam</u> was written, Thai women took great pride in preparing exotic dishes. Quiet competition to make the best-tasting meals exists among them to this day.

Nowhere else in the world are dishes given such intriguing names, coined to reflect their sensuous, subtle tastes. A dessert made from eggs, sugar, rice, and flour, soaked in hot syrup, is called "Golden Drop." The "Bed of Delight" is made from egg, pork, garlic, tamarind, red pepper, and parsley.

The people of Thailand prefer a light, spicy cuisine that will stimulate but not overburden the appetite in a hot, humid climate. Traditionally, meals are served on floor mats or on low tables surrounded by comfortable cushions. The Thais eat with a spoon held in the right hand and a fork in the left; chopsticks are often used for noodle dishes. Usually all the dishes in a meal, except dessert, are served at one time. The diners help themselves according to individual tastes.

Thai food, so expressive of the country's ornate nature, is always beautifully presented. It is, for example, Thai custom to sculpt fruit, and to garnish all their platters elaborately with sprigs of coriander, parsley, and other colorful herbs.

The recipes included here for your enjoyment are supplied by the personal chef of the Royal Family, Mr. Thanatsri Swaddiwatr. They are among the favorites of her Majesty, Queen Sirikit, who loves spicy food. Dinners at the Thai Embassy in Washington, D.C. are prepared and supervised by

Madame Revade Kasemsri, wife of Thailand's ambassador to the United States.

A dinner party at the Thai Embassy is one of the rarest treats in Washington, D.C. embassy entertaining. The buffet table is handsomely decorated, with flowers and fruits forming a brilliant background to the spread of luscious dishes.

At a Thai dinner the guests, upon arrival, are greeted by the host and hostess with a bow (a "Wai" in Thai) and the greeting: "Chean Krab"..."Welcome To My House."

## LAAB NUR SARANAE
### (Spicy Beef with Mint Leaves)

1 tablespoon rice flour
1 1/2 cups ground beef
1 tablespoon chopped red onion
3 cloves garlic
1 tablespooon nampla (fish sauce available in Asian grocery
  stores)
salt to taste
2 tablespoons fresh lemon or lime juice
1 teaspoon ground coriander seeds
1 teaspoon chili powder
1 tablespooon chopped green onion
10 mint leaves
lettuce leaves, green beans, and celery stalks, for garnish

1)  Preheat the oven to 325.

2)  Brown the rice flour by putting it in a small pan and heating it over low heat. Set it aside.

3)  Brown the ground beef, without using oil if possible, until it is no longer pink. Remove the meat from the skillet and place it in a mixing bowl; let it cool for 5 minutes.

4) Wrap the red onion and garlic in aluminum foil and heat them in the oven for at least 15 minutes, or until the onions are soft and translucent. Let them cool.

5)  Unwrap the red onion and garlic and pound them to a pulp; add this to the cooked ground beef.

6)  Season the beef with the nampla, salt, lemon or lime juice, coriander, chili, green onion, and the rice flour. Mix it thoroughly by hand.

7)  Put the beef mixture into the center of a serving plate, top it with the mint leaves, and garnish it with the raw vegetables.

### PAW PIER
(Spring Rolls)

*4 eggs, beaten lightly*
*2 1/4 teaspoons salt*
*2 cups plus 1 tablespoon vegetable oil*
*1/2 tablespoon chopped garlic*
*1 cup ground pork*
*1 tablespoon sugar*
*1/2 cup cooked small shrimp, chopped*
*1/2 cup cooked crab meat, flaked*
*1 cup bean sprouts*
*2 tablespoons chopped green onions*
*2 tablespoons chopped celery leaves*
*6 dried black mushrooms, boiled for 1/2 hour and chopped*
  *(optional)*
*1/2 cup glass noodles (mung bean vermicelli), soaked in water*
  *until soft*
*1 tablespoon soy sauce*
*1 tablespoon nampla (fish sauce available in Asian grocery*
*stores)*
*1 teaspoon pepper*
*12-14 egg roll wrappers, fresh or frozen*
*1 egg yolk, beaten lightly*

1) Add 1/4 teaspoon of the salt and 1 tablespoon of the oil to the eggs. Using a paper towel, oil a 10-inch frying pan. Heat the pan and pour in the eggs so that they cover the bottom in a thin layer. Cook them over low heat for about 5 minutes. When they are dry and slightly brown, remove them and cut them into long, very thin strips.

2) In a larger heavy skillet, heat 1 cup of the oil to hot but not smoking. Add the garlic and fry it for 2 minutes. Put in the ground pork, sugar, shrimp, crab meat, bean sprouts, green onions, celery, mushrooms, glass noodles, and egg strips. Toss and fry for 5 minutes. Add the soy sauce, the nampla, the rest of the salt, and the pepper.

3) Immerse the egg roll wrappers in warm water until they are pliable. Drain them briefly, then place about 2 tablespoons of the meat mixture on each one. Roll them, tucking in the sides as you roll, and seal them with a brush of beaten egg yolk.

4) Heat the remaining oil to hot but not smoking, and deep-fry the egg rolls for 5 to 10 minutes. Drain them on a paper towel. Serve hot.

### KUNG PUD BROCCOLI
Fried Broccoli With Shrimp

*6 jumbo shrimp*
*2 cups sliced broccoli (both stems and florets)*
*2 tablespoons vegetable oil*
*1 teaspoon minced garlic*
*1 teaspoon nampla (fish sauce available in Asian grocery stores)*
*1 tablespoon oyster sauce (also available in Asian grocery stores)*
*6 cups cooked rice, as an accompaniment*

1) Peel the shrimp and remove the black veins. Cut each one in half lengthwise, leaving one end attached, so that it looks like two shrimp. Soak the sliced broccoli in cold water for 15 minutes.

2) Heat the oil in a frying pan over medium heat. Fry the minced garlic until golden brown.

3) Add the sliced shrimp to the pan and fry, turning them over a few times. Add the nampla and the oyster sauce and stir-fry briefly. Drain the broccoli and add it to the pan; stir-fry for another 3 minutes. Spoon the shrimp and broccoli onto a serving plate and serve with the cooked rice.

### KALUM P.LEE
(Cabbage Salad)

*1 cup cabbage, finely chopped*
*3 cherry tomatoes, quartered*
*1/2 cup finely grated carrots*
*1 teaspoon garlic salt*
*2 tablespoons lime juice*
*1 teaspoon grated lime peel*
*1 teaspoon sugar, or to taste*
*2 or 3 hot chili peppers, pounded into small pieces*
*1 tablespoon dried shrimp, pounded into small pieces*

1) Mix the cabbage, tomatoes, and carrots, and season them with the garlic salt, lime juice, and lime peel. Add the sugar to taste.

2) Top the salad with the chili peppers and dried shrimp.

3) This is traditionally served on MALAGOH SOM TUM (papaya salad; see following page) as an accompaniment to KAI YANG (roast chicken; see following page).

## MALAGOH SOM TUM
### (Papaya Salad)

*1 cup peeled and finely chopped green papayas*
*3 cherry tomatoes, quartered*
*1 teaspoon garlic salt*
*2 tablespoons lime juice*
*1 teaspoon grated lime peel*
*1 teaspoon sugar, or to taste*
*2 or 3 hot chili peppers, pounded*
*1 tablespoon dried shrimp, pounded*

This recipe is made in the same fashion as KALUM PLEE (see previous page). Mix the papayas with the tomatoes, season with the garlic salt, lime juice, lime peel, and sugar, and top with the peppers and shrimp. To serve, place the KALUM PLEE (cabbage salad) on top of the MALAGOH SOM TUM (papaya salad); this accompanies the KAI YANG (roast chicken; see following page).

### KAI YANG
(Roasted Chicken)

*3 medium cloves garlic*
*1 teaspoon salt*
*1/2 teaspoon pepper*
*1 piece ginger (l-inch in diameter and 1/4-inch thick), minced*
*1 teaspoon minced coriander root*
*1 teaspoon vegetable oil*
*1 3-pound chicken, quartered*

1) Pound the garlic, salt, pepper, ginger, and coriander together and mix well with the vegetable oil.

2) Cover the chicken pieces well with this mixture and marinate them for 1 to 2 hours.

3) When ready to cook the chicken, preheat the oven to 375 and bake the chicken for 30 to 40 minutes.

4) Serve the chicken with the KALUM PLEE (cabbage salad) and/or the MALAGOH SOM TUM (papaya salad): see recipes on previous pages.

### SANG KAYA
(Custard Dessert)

*4 cups fresh coconut milk*
*2 cups palm sugar, or brown sugar*
*10 eggs, beaten*
*6 half coconut shells, optional*

1) Pour the coconut milk into the top of a large double boiler. Bring the water in the bottom to a boil, and then add the sugar to the coconut milk. Stir until it is dissolved.

2) Add the beaten eggs and blend well. Cover the custard and let it steam for about 45 minutes, until firm. Remove it from the heat and chill it until ready to serve.

3) If desired, the custard can be steamed in the half coconut shells (covered tightly with aluminum foil and placed in a large pot with 1-2 inches of water in the bottom) for 45 minutes, then chilled and served right in the shells.

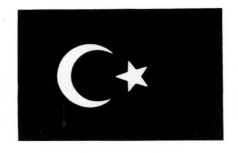

# THE EMBASSY OF THE REPUBLIC OF TURKEY

*Dinner for Six*

DUGUN CORBASI
*(Wedding Soup)*

CEVIZLI TAVUK
*(Chicken Walnut)*

FASULYE PILAKISI
*(White Kidney Beans Plaki)*

YALANCI DOLMA
*(Stuffed Grape Leaves)*

HUNKAR BEGENDI
*(Sultan's Delight)*

ISPANAKLI BOREK
*(Cheese and Spinach Borek)*

CO BAN SALATASI
*(Shepherds' Salad)*

SEKERPARE
*(Sugar Cookies)*

TAZE MEYVA
*(Fresh Fruit)*

TURK KAHVESI
*(Turkish Coffee)*

# REPUBLIC OF TURKEY

The Republic of Turkey spans two continents–Asia and Europe–and 10,000 years of the world's great cultures, history, and exotic beauty. Famous historical figures such as Homer, Mark Antony and Cleopatra, St. Paul, Hannibal, Persian King Xerxes, and the "Father of the Turks," Ataturk, have called Turkey home.

The imposing Embassy of the Republic of Turkey spans two main traffic arteries–Massachusetts Avenue and 23rd Street. High on a hill overlooking the city, the gray stone mansion, designed by a famous Turkish architect, houses treasures of the ancient and modern world: sumptuous Oriental rugs, classic bronzes, mahogany and teak panelling in the dining and ball rooms. In this opulent setting, Ambassador Doctor Sukru Elekdag and Madame Ayla Elekdag entertain lavishly at several dinners a week, carrying out the traditional Turkish hospitality; a guest in one's home is considered "a guest of God."

Turkish cuisine is famous for its rich variety of dishes and superb blending of spices and herbs. According to Turkish tradition, guests should enjoy at least five courses, starting with *mezes* (hors d'oeuvres), followed by soup, then meat served with *pilav* (rice) or *bulghur* (cracked wheat), a vegetable or two, and a salad. As a final touch, a tray of sweets and fresh, sun-ripened figs, grapes, and other fruits is served.

*Kahve* (Turkish coffee) ends the feast. Because of its rich aroma and taste, it is served in very small elegant cups. The Turks say that a cup of coffee can seal the bonds of a long friendship. Serious conversation between friends or business associates does not begin before coffee starts the flow of words.

*Kahve* (the basis of the English word) was introduced into Turkey by the Arabs, who would drink only the coffee prepared from the Yemen bean. It was roasted and freshly ground in very small quantities so that the rich flavor was not lost. Coffee was then brought to Europe in the sixteenth century by the Ottomans, and from Istanbul to Austria, from Vienna to Paris, the addiction to strong coffee extended to England.

Another national drink is *raki*, an anisette-flavored spirit made from *arak* (as is *ouzo*) and served instead of wine, with dinner. A Turkish *raki* dinner often lasts three hours.

As for sweets, many people assume the croissant originated in France, but they are wrong. Austrian cooks first created these pastries when the Turks invaded their country; they borrowed the shape from the design on the Turkish flag. The Austrians still make their croissants in that shape, and the French, and now the Americans.

While the Turkish Embassy dinners in Washington are very elegant, with delicate crystal, gold and white flatware, candles, and embroidered table linens, the same dinner in a village of Turkey might be served at a low table, the guests seated on cushions on the floor.

At the start or the end of the meal, it is customary to hear "Afiyet Olsun," which means: "May what you eat become part of you in strength and health." To compliment the cook for a delicious meal, one says "Elinize saglik"..."Bless your hands."

But the toast is the same in Istanbul and the villages of Turkey as it is in the splendid embassy in Washington: "Sherefe"..."To Your Health."

## DUGUN  CORBASI
(Wedding Soup)

2 pounds lamb bones, with some meat on them
5 cups water
salt to taste
1 medium onion, quartered
1 medium carrot, halved
8 tablespoons butter
1/2 cup unbleached flour
2 egg yolks, beaten
juice of 1/2 lemon
1/8 teaspoon cayenne pepper
3/4 tablespoon paprika
croutons

1) Put the lamb bones, water, salt, onion, and carrot in a 2 1/2-quart saucepan and cook for an hour over medium heat.

2) Strain the soup.  Discard the onion and carrot; remove any meat from the bones and add it to the broth.

3) In another large saucepan, melt 6 tablespoons of the butter over low heat.  Whisk in the flour and stir constantly for 5-7 minutes, making a roux.

4) Gradually add the meat stock to the roux, stirring constantly. Simmer this mixture for 10 minutes over low heat, then remove it from the heat but keep it warm.

5) While beating the egg yolks, add the lemon juice slowly, then gradually stir in 2 tablespoons of the warm stock.  Now pour this egg mixture into the soup, stirring constantly.  If the soup is thicker than you desire, stir in a little hot water.

6) Melt the last 2 tablespoons of butter in a small pan and sprinkle in the cayenne and paprika.

7) To serve, pour the hot soup into bowls. Add an equal amount of the spiced butter mixture to each bowl, and top with croutons.

### CEVIZLI TAVUK
(Chicken Walnut)

1  3 1/2-pound chicken
2 quarts water
1 large stalk celery, cut into 5 pieces
1 large carrot, scaped and cut into 4 pieces
1 large onion, quartered
4 sprigs parsley
salt and pepper to taste
3 thin slices white bread, crusts removed
2 cups shelled walnuts, finely chopped
1 large clove of garlic, crushed
1 tablespoon oil
1 teaspoon paprika

1) Wash the chicken and place it in a 5-quart saucepan with the water, celery, carrot, onion, parsley, salt, and pepper. Bring it to a boil and skim off the foam. Cover the pan and cook over medium heat until the chicken is tender–about 1 1/2 hours.

2) Remove the chicken and let it cool. Strain the stock and save it. Discard the vegetables.

3) Remove the skin from the chicken and the meat from the bones. Cut the meat into 2- or 3-inch chunks and set it aside.

4) Soak the bread in the chicken stock, then squeeze it until it is fairly dry. Put it into a food processor with the chopped walnuts and more salt and pepper if desired. Add the crushed garlic and process at medium speed until everything is thoroughly mixed.

5) With the processor running, add chicken stock until the mixture is the consistency of mayonnaise. This could take a cup or more. Transfer this sauce to a bowl.

6) Mix the chicken pieces with 1/4 of the sauce and put them on a serving platter. Then spread the rest of the sauce smoothly over the chicken.

7) Heat the oil in a small pan over low heat. Add the paprika but do not stir; continue to heat until the oil becomes red in color. Pour the red oil over the chicken, leaving the paprika in the saucepan.

## FASULYE PILAKISI
### (White Kidney Beans Plaki)

1 cup dry white kidney beans, soaked overnight
3 cups of water
salt to taste
4 medium white onions, diced
2 medium tomatoes, diced
1 medium carrot, diced
2 medium stalks celery, diced
2 medium cloves garlic, finely chopped
1/4 cup olive oil
1 medium potato, diced
2 tablespoons lemon juice
pinch of cayenne pepper
1/2 teaspoon sugar
1/2 lemon, thinly sliced
1 tablespoon fresh parsley, chopped

1) Put the beans, water, and salt in a 2-quart saucepan. Bring to a boil and cook over medium heat for 15 minutes.

2) Transfer the beans to a 3-quart saucepan and add the diced onion, tomato, carrot, and celery, and the garlic and oil. Mix well and add water if necessary to cover the beans and vegetables. Cover the pot and cook over medium heat for 30 minutes.

3) Add the potato, lemon juice, cayenne, and sugar; cover and cook over medium heat until the beans are tender, about 20 minutes more. More water may be added as the dish should not be too dry.

4) The beans should be served on a platter, garnished with the lemon slices and chopped parsley.

## YALANCI DOLMA
### (Stuffed Grape Leaves)

6 cups water
1 16-ounce jar grape leaves, stems intact
1/4 cup fresh parsley
1/4 cup fresh dill
2 large white onions, coarsely grated
1 cup rice
1/4 cup fresh mint, chopped
3 tablespoons black currants
2 tablespoons pignoli nuts
1 tablespoon allspice
2/3 cup olive oil
1 teaspoon sugar
2 tablespoons lemon juice
salt to taste
2 cups chicken broth
2 lemons, cut into wedges

1) Bring the water to a roiling boil in a 4-quart saucepan. Unroll the grape leaves and put them in the boiling water; cook for 2 minutes.

2) Remove the leaves with a slotted spoon and place them in a colander to drain. Try not to let them overlap.

3) Chop the parsley and dill; reserve the stems. These should be distributed evenly in the bottom of a heavy 9 by 12-inch flameproof pan.

4) Put into a mixing bowl the following: parsley, dill, onions, rice, mint, currants, pignolis, allspice, oil, sugar, lemon juice, and salt. Mix well with your hands.

5) To stuff the dolmas, place each leaf on a flat surface, smooth side down and stem toward you. Put 1 heaping teaspoon of the rice mixture on the stem end. Fold the stem over and begin to roll. After one revolution tuck the sides in; continue rolling to the end of the leaf. Divide the mixture so as to have around six dolmas per guest.

6) Place the dolmas side by side on top of the dill and parsley stems. If necessary, make two layers.

7) Pour the chicken broth over the dolmas and cover the pan with aluminum foil. Pat it down firmly. Two or three layers of foil may be used to add weight to hold it in place. Cook the dolmas over medium heat until the rice is tender and the water is absorbed, about 1 hour. (It may be necessary to add more water.) Remove the pan from the heat and allow the dolmas to cool, covered.

8) Put the dolmas on a serving platter and garnish them with lemon wedges.

## HUNKAR BEGENDI
### (Sultan's Delight)

*1 1/2 pounds lamb, cut into 1-inch cubes*
*2 small onions, chopped*
*2 tablespoons butter*
*2 small tomatoes, diced*
*salt and pepper to taste*
*1 tablespoon parsley, chopped*
*BEGENDI (eggplant puree; see following page)*

1)  Place the meat, onions, and butter in a 3-quart saucepan and saute over medium heat, stirring occasionally, until the meat turns brown--about 10 minutes.

2)  Add the tomatoes and saute for 5 more minutes. Season with the salt and pepper, then cover the saucepan and cook the meat over low heat until it is tender, about 1 hour. Test it with a fork. If necessary, add a little warm water during the cooking time.

3)  Place the meat on a round serving platter and put the BEGENDI (see following page) around it. Garnish with the parsley. Serve hot.

**BEGENDI**
(Eggplant Puree)

*juice of 1 lemon*
*5 cups cold water*
*salt to taste*
*6 medium eggplants*
*4 tablespoons butter*
*2 tablespoons flour*
*1 cup warm milk*
*1/2 cup grated cheddar cheese*

1) Mix the lemon juice, salt, and cold water in a bowl. Set aside.

2) Cut several slits in each eggplant, inserting a knife about 1 to 1 1/2 inches. Roast each eggplant directly over a gas or electric burner on high, holding it on a long fork and turning it until the skin is black all around and the insides are soft.

3) When the eggplants are done, peel them and remove the seeds. Put the pulp into the lemon juice mixture.

4) Melt the butter in a 3- or 4-quart saucepan. Whisk in the flour and cook over medium heat, stirring constantly, until the flour turns a light golden brown–about 5 minutes. Stir in the warm milk gradually.

5) Squeeze the water from the eggplant pulp and chop it into small pieces. Add them to the saucepan, with the grated cheese. Using a potato masher, reduce this mixture to a smooth pasty consistency. Cook it over medium heat until bubbles form-- about 10 minutes. Serve with the meat as described above.

## ISPANAKLI BOREK
### (Cheese and Spinach Borek)

1 10-ounce package frozen chopped spinach
3 tablespoon olive oil
1 large white onion, grated
4 tablespoons Parmesan cheese, grated
3 tablespoons feta cheese, crumbled
1/2 tablespoon sugar
salt and pepper to taste
3 eggs, lightly beaten
4 tablespoons milk
12 tablespoons butter, melted
1 pound phyllo dough (available frozen)

1) To prepare the filling, thaw the spinach, squeeze out any moisture, and set it aside. Heat the oil in a 10-inch skillet and saute the onion for 8 minutes over medium heat, stirring occasionally. Remove the pan from the heat and add the spinach, two cheeses, sugar, salt, pepper, eggs, and milk. Mix well by hand.

2) Preheat the oven to 350.

3) Brush an 18 by 12-inch baking pan with some of the melted butter. Divide the pound of phyllo into six equal portions (there should be five or six sheets in each).

4) Lay one pastry sheet from each of the six portions on a smooth surface and brush it lightly with butter. Do not leave puddles. Put a second sheet on the first one and brush it with butter. Continue this until each sheet in each pile has been buttered. When you are finished, there will be six piles of the layered buttered sheets.

5) Divide the spinach mixture into 6 equal portions. Place each one in a straight line on one of the piles of phyllo sheets, about 5 inches from the edge. Fold the sheets over the filling and roll them up like a strudel pastry.

6) When the six rolls are finished, place them in the buttered pan and brush them with any remaining melted butter. Bake them about 30 minutes, or until golden brown. Serve hot.

### CO BAN SALATASI
(Shepherds' Salad)

*4 leaves romaine*
*1/2 head boston lettuce*
*1 medium tomato*
*1 green pepper, seeded*
*1/2 large cucumber*
*2 scallions or green onions (including tops)*
*2 red radishes*
*2 tablespoons fresh mint, chopped*
*2 tablespoons fresh dill, chopped*
*2 tablespoons fresh parsley, chopped*
*6 slices of roasted red pepper*
*6 green olives*

*LEMON SAUCE:*

*2 tablespoons lemon juice*
*3 tablespoons olive oil*
*1 tablespoon wine vinegar*

1) Make the lemon sauce by combining all the ingredients in a bowl and mixing by hand.

2) Thinly slice the romaine, lettuce, tomato, green pepper, cucumber, scallions, and radishes.  Toss them in a large bowl with the mint, dill, and parsley.

3) Add the lemon sauce to the greens according to taste.  Put equal amounts of salad on each of six plates, and garnish each with a red pepper slice and an olive.


## SEKERPARE
### (Sugar Cookies)

*2 cups granulated sugar*
*2 1/2 cups water*
*1 tablespoon lemon juice*
*1 egg, beaten lightly*
*3/4 cup powdered sugar*
*1 cup margarine, melted and cooled*
*1 teaspoon salt*
*1/2 teaspoon baking soda*
*5 cups all-purpose flour*
*15 almonds, skinned by soaking in hot water*

1) Make a honey syrup by boiling the sugar, water, and lemon juice for 20 minutes.  Set it aside to cool.

2) Preheat the oven to 350.

3) In a large bowl, mix the egg with the powdered sugar.  Add the cooled margarine and beat for 5 minutes.

4) Combine the salt, baking soda, and flour. Add this to the egg mixture, stir well, and knead it for about 10 minutes, until a dough forms.

5) Roll the dough into balls (about one tablespoon each) between the palms of your hands. Then flatten them to 1/4-inch thickness and place them on a greased cookie sheet.

6) Press an almond into the top of each cookie.

7) Bake the cookies for 35-40 minutes, or until lightly browned. While they are still hot, dip them into the cool honey syrup, then place them on a serving dish.

### TURK KAHVESI
(Turkish Coffee)

*6 demitasse cupfuls cold water*
*6 teaspoons pulverized Turkish coffee (see note)*
*6 teaspoons sugar (or less, according to taste)*

1) For each serving, put 1 cupful of water into the *jezve* (see note). Add 1 teaspoon of coffee and 1 of sugar and stir well. Over low heat, bring the coffee just to the boil. Remove it from the heat immediately, stir it once, and pour the froth off into the demitasse cup.

2) Put the coffee back on the heat and bring it to the boil again. Stir once more and fill the cup.

Note: Turkish coffee is made in a cylindrical pot with a long handle, called a *jezve*, which is sold in most department stores and in shops specializing in Eastern Mediterranean foods. It comes in various sizes; the 4-cup is recommended as it can be used for 1, 2, 3, or 4 cups. Pulverized coffee can also be obtained from specialty-food shops. Also, some shops will pulverize coffee if the customer requests Turkish coffee.

# THE EMBASSY OF THE
## SOCIALIST FEDERAL REPUBLIC OF YUGOSLAVIA

*Dinner for Ten*

### RAKOVI
*(Cooked Shrimp with Lemon Sauce)*

### ZELJANICA
*(Crusty Spinach Souffle Pie)*

### SARMA PROJA
*(Stuffed Cabbage with Cornbread)*

### CURKA CREVENI KUPUS
*(Roast Turkey with Stewed Red Cabbage)*

### PREBRANAC PECENO PRASE
*(Roast Suckling Pig with Baked Lima Beans)*

### URNEBES SALATA
*(Hubbub Salad)*

### SALATA OD BORANIJE
*(French Bean Salad)*

### MIMOSA SALAD

### POGACA
*(Peasant Bread)*

### PITA OD JABUKA
*(Apple Cake)*

Madame Mico Rakic, the wife of the Yugoslav ambassador to the United States, welcomed her guests in the large, cream-colored drawing room of the ambassador's residence on R Street in Washington, D. C. After showing us around the elegant, panelled room, with its brilliant oil paintings by Berber and other Yugoslavian artists, she served us champagne, white wine, caviar, and rich fruit-filled pastries, which, she said, "I personally made for you last night."

Ambassador and Mrs. Rakic have been in Washington for two years. Previous postings have included East Africa, Uganda, and Berundi. The ambassador also served for six years in Yugoslavia as a member of the President's staff. Before coming to the United States, he held the Cabinet post of Deputy Secretary for Foreign Affairs.

Madame Rakic loves to entertain and enjoys giving formal dinners, often for twenty-four to twenty-eight guests. To promote a more friendly atmosphere, she seats seven or eight to a table. Each table is beautifully set with crystal, displayed on lace tablecloths handmade in Yugoslavia.

In arranging for the many luncheons and dinners, Madame Rakic is helped by Katarina Linta, one of the few female chefs serving in a Washington diplomatic setting. She has been with the Yugoslavian Embassy for several years. Her husband is maitre d'hotel and general supervisor.

Madame Rakic becomes animated about Yugolsavian cookery and its origins. With great emotion she points out that her home is a country of contrasts in climate, culture, and vegetation. "The Yugoslavs," she explains, "speak three separate languages, have two alphabets, and three religions. And," she continues, "we are bordered by Italy, Austria, Hungary, Romania, Bulgaria, Albania, and the Adriatic Sea. It is not surprising that our cookery is diverse and cosmopolitan."

Yugoslav cuisine is a fascinating melange of varied foods. In Macedonia, Islamic and Turkish dishes featuring lamb are served, as are Greek dishes such as *moussaka*. The Serbians, with Balkan and Hungarian influences, enjoy heavily-spiced foods, and favor pork over lamb. The Slovenes, close to Italy and once part of the Austrian-Hungarian Empire, love pasta. They are particularly proud of their pastries and cakes. Montenegro, influenced by Venice, features seafood, grilled dishes, and lamb specialties.

One of the strongest marks on this country's cooking was left by five centuries of Turkish rule. Yugoslavs still enjoy an array of appetizers call _meze_--small pieces of fried liver, white and yellow goat cheese, nuts, fruits, pickled vegetables, and small cheese-filled pastries. With these, guests are served _slivovitz_, the national drink--a clear, potent, plum brandy.

After sampling many of these spicy delicacies, we sat down with Madame Rakic and the Press Counselor, delightful Mr. Ljubomir Vujic, and outlined a dinner party buffet. That menu is offered here for your enjoyment. If you like, you can prepare a smaller dinner using only selected dishes. You will find each course to be an interesting and exotic contrast, the result of the unique combinations of peoples, customs, climates, and foods that constitute the Socialist Federal Republic of Yugoslavia.

"Ziveli!"..."To Long Life!"

# SOCIALIST FEDERAL REPUBLIC OF YUGOSLAVIA

## RAKOVI
### (Cooked Shrimp with Lemon Sauce)

*2 pounds medium-size shrimp*
*1/2 cup red wine*
*1/2 cup water*
*2 tablespoons parsley, finely chopped*
*1 1/2 ounces capers, finely chopped*
*juice of 2 lemons*
*1/2 cup olive oil*
*1/2 cup vegetable oil*
*1 tablespoon mustard*
*salt and pepper to taste*
*3 1/2 ounces black olives, for garnish*

1) Place the shrimp in a deep pot. Add the wine and water; cook for 10 minutes. Drain the shrimp, reserving 1/2 cup of the broth. Peel and devein the shrimp and mix them with the parsley and capers.

2) Make the sauce by mixing the reserved broth with the lemon juice, oils, mustard, salt, and pepper. Pour 2/3 of this over the shrimp and refrigerate them for 24 hours, covered.

3) Before serving, place the olives on the shrimp; top with the remaining sauce.

### ZELJANICA
(Crusty Spinach Souffle Pie)

*2 pounds phyllo dough (available frozen at many food stores)*
*6 eggs*
*l pound feta cheese*
*1 pound creamed cottage cheese*
*1 pound cream cheese*
*1 pound spinach, cooked, drained, and chopped*
*2 cups whole milk*
*1 cup vegetable oil*

1) Thaw the phyllo and allow it to reach room temperature before proceeding.

2) Preheat the oven to 400.

3) Beat the eggs and blend in the feta, using a potato masher to break it up. Add the cottage cheese, cream cheese, spinach, and milk; mix well.

4) Grease a large baking pan (about 10 inches in diameter and 4 inches deep) with oil. Lay three or four sheets of phyllo into the pan, letting the edges hang over. Sprinkle them with oil and then with a little water.

5) Place about 1 1/2 cups of the cheese filling onto the phyllo and cover it with three or four more sheets; again sprinkle it with oil and water. Repeat these steps until all the filling is used. Top the pie with four more sheets of phyllo and sprinkle them with oil only. Tuck the edges of the overhanging phyllo sheets in under the pie.

6) Bake the pie for 45 minutes, then reduce the oven temperature to 350 and cook for an additional 15 minutes. The zeljanica is done when the crust is golden brown, and a knife inserted in the center comes out clean.

7) Remove the pie from the oven and run a knife or spatula around the edges so that they do not stick. Serve warm.


### SARMA PROJA
#### (Stuffed Cabbage with Corn Bread)

*1 3-pound head cabbage*
*salt to taste*
*2 pounds fresh pork*
*1/4 pound cooked ham*
*1/4 pound fresh beef*
*1 pound bacon*
*1 large onion, chopped*
*2 tablespoons lard*
*1 teaspoon salt*
*1/2 teaspoon pepper*
*5 tablespoons cooked white rice*
*1 egg, beaten*
*1 pound sauerkraut*
*2 large fresh or canned tomatoes, chopped*
*2 tablespoons flour, dissolved in 3/4 cup water*
*PROJA (corn bread; see below)*

1) Boil a pot of water, salted to taste. Remove the pot from the flame and put in the head of cabbage. Let it stand, covered, for one hour. Meanwhile, grind all the meats together.

2) Brown the onion in the lard. Add the ground meat, salt, pepper, rice, and egg; mix well. Remove the cabbage from the water and cut out the core. Taking one leaf at a time, place a tablespoon of the filling in the center and roll the leaf, turning the edges in so the meat will not ooze out. You may use toothpicks to hold the rolls together.

3) Preheat the oven to 350.

4) Arrange the stuffed leaves in the bottom of a roasting pan and cover them with sauerkraut. Make a second or third layer of leaves and sauerkraut if necessary. Add water to cover, and sprinkle with the tomatoes. Bake, uncovered, for 2 hours.

5) Before serving, remove the cabbage rolls and make a gravy with the liquid in the pan, thickening it with the flour dissolved in water. Pour this over the cabbage rolls and serve immediately, with PROJA (see following page).

## SOCIALIST FEDERAL REPUBLIC OF YUGOSLAVIA

### PROJA
### (Corn Bread)


*1 1/2 pounds corn meal*
*4 eggs*
*1 cup oil*
*1 cup melted butter*
*1 cup creamed cottage cheese*
*1/2 cup milk*
*1/2 cup sour cream*
*1 cup club soda*


1)  Preheat the oven to 450.

2)  Mix all the ingredients until blended.  Pour the batter into a greased 6 by 8-inch baking pan and bake for about 30 minutes, or until golden brown.

3)  Serve the corn bread warm, with the stuffed cabbage rolls.


### CURKA CREVENI KUPUS
### (Roast Turkey with Stewed Red Cabbage)


*10 or 12-pound turkey*
*salt and pepper to taste*
*onion powder, garlic powder, and dried parsley to taste*
*1/4 cup oil*
*2 cups chicken bouillon*

1) Sprinkle the turkey, inside and out, with the seasonings. refrigerate it for 24 hours.

2) Preheat the oven to 400.

3) Heat the oil. Place the turkey in a roasting pan and pour the oil over it. Roast it at 400 for half an hour, then turn the heat down to 300 and continue roasting for 3 1/2 to 4 1/2 hours (about 20 minutes per pound), basting it with the bouillon and the turkey drippings.

4) Serve the turkey surrounded by CREVENI  KUPUS (stewed red cabbage; see following  page).

# SOCIALIST FEDERAL REPUBLIC OF YUGOSLAVIA

**CREVENI KUPUS**
(Stewed Red Cabbage)

3 1/2 pounds red cabbage
1 tablespoon sugar
salt and white pepper to taste
1 cup oil
1 cup white wine
1 ounce red wine vinegar

1) Grate the cabbage or mince it in a food processor. Add the sugar, salt, and pepper; mix well. Cover it and let it stand for 2 hours.

2) Warm the oil in a large pan. Add the cabbage. Bring it to a simmer, then add the wine and cook it for about 15 minutes, or until the cabbage is soft. Add the vinegar and cook it for another 5 minutes.

3) Serve the cabbage surrounding the roast turkey.

### PREBRANAC PECENO PRASE
(Roast Suckling Pig with Baked Lima Beans)

*10 to l5-pound suckling pig*
*salt to taste*
*1 clean quart bottle*
*1 large walnut*
*1 cup oil*
*1 12-ounce bottle light beer*

1)  Preheat the oven to 400.

2)  Rub the inside of the pig thoroughly with salt.  Place the quart bottle into the cavity and truss the pig.  Place the walnut between the pig's jaws.  These will help the pig keep its shape during roasting.

3) Dry the pig well with a paper towel and rub the outside thoroughly with salt.  Place the pig in a roasting pan with four small boards underneath to prevent sticking.  Pour the oil over the pig and roast it for about 5 hours, basting it frequently with the beer and drippings.

4) Serve the pig cold with PREBANAC (baked lima beans; see following page) and salad.

## PREBANAC
### (Baked Lima Beans)

*2 pounds large dried lima beans*
*salt to taste*
*2 or 3 bay leaves*
*1 1/2 cups oil*
*3 pounds red onions, finely chopped*
*2 tablespoons paprika*
*1 tablespoon pepper*

1) Soak the beans overnight in water to cover. When ready to cook them, drain them, pour on fresh water to cover, and heat them to a boil. Drain them again and again add fresh cold water, plus the salt and bay leaves. Cook them for about 1 1/2 hours, or until soft.

2) In the meantime, heat the oil and brown the onions slightly. Add the paprika and pepper.

3) Preheat the oven to 350.

4) Mix the beans with the onions. Place them in a casserole dish 8 inches in diameter and 5 inches deep. Bake them for 35 minutes, or until the top is golden brown. Remove the bay leaves before serving.

### URNEBES SALATA
(Hubbub Salad)

*10 sweet red peppers*
*6 hot peppers*
*2 eggplants*
*1 pound feta cheese*
*2 cloves garlic, crushed*
*3 yolks of hard-boiled eggs, mashed*
*2 teaspoons paprika*
*2 tablespoons wine vinegar, or to taste*
*1/2 cup oil, corn or olive*

1) Preheat the oven to 350.

2) Roast the peppers for 15 minutes and the eggplants for 20 minutes, or until soft. Peel the vegetables and chop them finely.

3) With a fork, mash the feta to a paste. Add the chopped vegetables and the garlic, egg yolks, paprika, and vinegar. Mix these well and arrange them on a serving plate. Pour the oil over the salad and serve.

### SALATA OD BORANIJE
(French Bean Salad)

2 pounds string beans
3 tablespoons wine vinegar
6 tablespoons olive oil
1/2 clove garlic, minced
3 tablespoons chopped parsley
salt and pepper to taste

Boil the beans in salted water for 15 minutes. Drain them. While they are still warm, add the vinegar, oil, garlic, parsley, salt, and pepper. Mix well and put into a serving bowl.

### MIMOSA SALAD

2-3 heads lettuce, of different varieties if desired
salt to taste
1/2 cup oil
2-3 tablespoons wine vinegar
2 yolks of hard-boiled eggs, crushed

Shred the lettuce. Wash it, salt it, and place it in a bowl. Mix the oil and vinegar and dress the salad with it right before serving. Sprinkle the egg yolks over the salad for garnish.

## POGACA
(Peasant Bread)

*1 1/2 pounds self-rising flour*
*1/2 cup plus 2 tablespoons olive oil*
*1/2 teaspoon salt*
*1 cup plain carbonated water*

1)  Preheat the oven to 400.

2)  Combine the flour with 1/2 cup of the oil and the salt.  Add the carbonated water until a soft dough is formed.  Knead it well, adding more flour if necessary.  With a rolling pin, spread the dough into a flat circle about 9 inches in diameter and 1 1/2 inches thick.  Sprinkle the remaining oil on both sides.

3) Using a sharp knife, make cuts about an inch apart, crisscrossing the dough.

4) Place the dough on a greased cookie sheet or greased aluminum foil on the center rack of the oven.  Bake it for about 45 minutes, or until it is golden brown.

### PITA OD JABUKA
#### (Apple Cake)

*7 eggs, separated*
*13 ounces sugar*
*3 1/2 ounces ground walnuts*
*2 tablespoons dry cream of wheat cereal*
*juice and grated rind of 1 orange*
*25 ounces flour*
*2 cups whole milk*
*juice of 3 lemons, plus grated rind of one*
*5-6 large sour apples*
*orange slices for garnish*

1)  Preheat the oven to 350.

2)  To make the dough, beat three of the egg yolks with 4 ounces of the sugar.  Add the walnuts, cream of wheat, and orange juice and rind.  When this is well blended, gently fold in three of the egg whites, stiffly beaten.  Spread the dough into a greased 8  by 10-inch baking pan, and bake for 30 minutes.

3) To make the cream filling, beat the four remaining egg yolks and another 4 ounces of the sugar until smooth.  Add the flour and blend well.  Then add the milk and the juice and rind of one lemon.  Put this mixture in the top of a double boiler and cook, stirring, until it is thick–about 15 to 20 minutes.

4)  To make the apple filling, peel and core the apples, and then grate them.  Simmer them with the juice of one lemon until all the liquid is absorbed.

5)  Preheat the oven to 300.

6) To make the meringue topping, beat the four remaining egg whites, gradually adding the juice of the last lemon and the remaining 5 ounces of sugar. Beat until stiff.

7) To assemble the dessert, place the baked dough into a mold, spread the cream filling over it, spread the apple filling over that, and then top it with the meringue. Bake it for 40 minutes, or until the meringue is lightly browned.

8) Chill the cake for 24 hours. To serve it, unmold it onto a serving plate and garnish it with orange slices.

The following list is a brief description of each spice or herb used by the embassies in their recipies. (Excluding salt and pepper).

**Allspice** is derived from the Jamaica pepper *(evergreen pimenta)* and from the seeds of the nigella plants family. The seeds from these plants, themselves sometimes called "devil-in-the-bush," are often used as pepper. Allspice combines the flavor of cinnamon, nutmeg, cloves, and traces of other similar spices. It is used in making pickles, chutney, ketchup, in seasoning poultry and sausages, and in cakes and pies.

**Asafetida** is a soft, brown, lumpy, gum-like resin having an acid taste and a very strong, almost objectionable odor. It is derived from the roots of a plant of the carrot family. It is often called "devil's dung."

**Basil** is a tropical plant of which there are over fifty differing species. It is a member of the mint family. The more common varieties are sweet basil, monk's basil, and bush basil. Basil was once considered a plant for sovereigns' exclusive use, harvested only with a golden sickle. It is used to sweeten tomatoes, poultry, soups, salads, some meats, and can be used in wine or cider vinegar.

**Bay leaves** are of the laurel family and in ancient times, were formed into a wreath which was used to crown the victorious in battle. The bay leaf is an integral part of the "bouquet garni," a mixture of herbs tied together and used to flavor soup, meat, and fish. Bay leaves are also used alone and are especially desirable when cooking shrimp.

**Cardamom** is a blend of peppergrass and "amomom," an Indian spice plant. It is a member of the ginger family, and its aromatic seeds are used both in medicine and as a condiment. In Arabic countries, cardamom is often used to flavor coffee.

**Cayenne pepper** comes from the very hot members of the pepper family, of which there are over 100 varieties. The more common kinds of these chili peppers are the Japanese and the Mexican chilis. Both are very hot and should be used sparingly. Cayenne is the ground version of these peppers and is an unforgettable addition to sauces, soups, and meat and vegetable dishes.

**Chives** are a perennial herb allied to the leek and onion family. Though used chiefly to season green salads, chives are also used to add a mild onion flavor to soups, omelettes, and fish.

**Cinnamon** is derived from the bark of the evergreen cassia tree. The best of this exotic spice comes from Viet Nam, although it is also cultivated in other tropical countries. It comes powdered, and in thin sticks of rolled pieces of bark that can be up to a yard in length. It is naturally yellowish in color and has a sweet, hot taste. (Powdered cinnamon is sometimes dried, the essential oils extracted, and subject to many other adulterations.)

**Citron** is a species of lemon with a thick skin, and is cultivated on the Mediterranean coast. The perfumed fruit is seldom eaten fresh, but is used largely in making cakes and confectionary. In Corsica a liqueur called *cedratine* is made from this fruit.

**Cloves** come from the flower of the evergreen clove tree and are thought to have originated in China. They are picked while in bud, dried in the sun and resemble a nail, hence their name which is derived from the Latin "clavus"– nail. Across the years clove trees found their way into the Moluccas, Mauritius, and into Cayenne and Zanzibar in the West Indies. Cloves are highly aromatic and spicy hot in flavor. They are used in making pickles, canning, and in baking.

**Coriander** is the small fruit of a plant related to the carrot family. Light yellowish brown in color and aromatic, its taste is bittersweet. Coriander is used to flavor cheeses, and some sausages, meats, soups, and salads. It is also used in certain spirits.

**Cream of Tartar** is a crystalline substance, white, and with an acidulous taste. It is an ingredient of baking powder.

**Cumin** is used extensively in chilis and curry dishes as a basic ingredient. It is a long, spindle-shaped seed, dull yellow or light brown in color. It is acrid and spicy and should be added with caution. Cumin is used is making some cheeses, Munster especially, and to flavor spaghetti.

**Curry**, usually associated with Indian cuisine, is a mixture of dried spices, as few as five or as many as fifty. The more common variety contains allspice, anise, bay leaves, cinnamon, caraway, celery seed, cloves, coriander, cumin, curry leaves, dill fennel, fenugreek, garlic, ginger, mace, mustard, nutmeg, pepper, paprika, poppy seed, saffron, turmeric, mint cubeb berries, sumach seeds, juniper berries, zedoary root, and salt. Curry powder can be added to fish, meat, eggs, and vegetables.

**Dill** is the seeds or leaves of an annual of the parsley family. It has long-stocked umbels of yellow flowers and is aromatic and pungent. Dill leaves are used to flavor fish, cheese, and eggs, as well as salads. The seeds are often used in pickling; in fruit pies such as apple; and in beets, soups, and sauerkraut.

**Garlic**—the most widely used seasoning in this book—is the bulb of a perennial plant. Garlic was once worshipped, and Mohammed said of garlic "In cases of stings and bites by poisonous animals, garlic acts as a theriac. Applied to the spot bitten by viper, or sting of scorpion, it produces successful effects." The wonderful herb is served in many forms: garlic butter, in oil, powdered, in puree, sauces, on toast, and there is even garlic soup.

**Ginger** is the root of a tropical plant originally grown in Bengal and Malibar. There are two kinds: gray, which is the strongest, and comes in tubercles with grayish-yellow skin and pronounced rings; and white, which is solid skinned. Ginger has been used in cooking throughout recorded history. Grated, it seasons meat, poultry, and soups. Oriental cuisine is seldom without the zest lent by ginger root.

**Lemon grass** is a tropical grass growing in small tubular stocks like green onions. The leaves are long and tough and the bunches range in size up to about 1 inch or so in diameter. It has a sour taste and is used in flavoring soups, and many oriental dishes, but is usually removed before serving.

**Lotus** is one of the Old World plants of the waterlily family. It is noted for its large floating leaves and flamboyant flower. In ancient Egypt the lotus was eaten grilled or boiled. "Lotus eater" was a name given to those who lived in irresponsible enjoyment or sexual indulgence which was believed to result from eating the lotus plant.

**Marjoram** is any of several perennial herbs of the mint family. It is an aromatic herb that flowers in the middle of summer. Sweet marjoram (as opposed to oregano) can be used in all kinds of cooking but is not suitable for desserts.

**Mint** grows in many varieties. It was once thought to arouse latent passions, and military leaders, whom rulers wanted chaste, were not allowed to use it. The more common are spearmint and peppermint. Common mint is a small, green plant growing best in relatively moist, shady places. It is refreshingly aromatic, especially when the leaves are crushed. Mint is sometimes used in cooking chicken and pork. Oriental foods rely heavily on the leaves to flavor many dishes based on pork and beef. Mint sauce is a must when serving lamb.

**Nampla** is a fish sauce used commonly in Thailand, Viet Nam, Laos, and China. It has a very strong odor that some find objectionable. However, used in proper amounts—it has a great deal of salt in it—it adds a unique flavor to meat, vegetables, and rice dishes.

# SPICES & SEASONINGS

**Nutmeg** is the kernel of the fruit of evergreens growing in the Molucca Islands. It is oval in shape and grayish-brown in color; it has a whitish coating of milk of lime. The kernal is twenty-five percent nutmeg butter, a very aromatic and volatile fat. The kernals should be ground fresh since the palate-stimulating oils quickly dissipate. This widely used spice is a must for custard and egg nog and is also used with fruit cakes, some pastries, and soup.

**Oregano**, called wild majoram, is an extremely potent herb. It has a most pungent smell and slightly bitter taste. It is perhaps the variety of majoram most used in Italian, Mexican, Spanish, and Greek cooking. Oregano may be substituted for majoram, but the two should never be used together. Oregano adds a deep flavor to tomato sauces. In preparing salad dressing it should be used very lightly. (Ancients believed that a cocktail made from white wine and oregano was a sure cure for snake bites.)

**Oyster sauce** is a blend of oyster extract, brine, starch, other compounds, and colored with caramel. It has a delicate oyster flavor, is the consistency of slightly heavy cream, and is excellent on green vegetables, especially French (string) beans. Widely used in the orient, it is also fundamental to certain meat dishes such as beef and pork.

**Paprika**, the Hungarian name for sweet red pepper, has been used with great favor by cooks for centuries. Hailed as a magic herb, it is singularly responsible for the magnificent flavor Hungarian cooks give to chicken and goulashes.

**Parsley**, after garlic, is the most commonly used herb. It is part of the umbelliferous family and had finely divided leaves and a greenish-yellow flower. It has an acid-sweet taste and is basic to every bouquet garni. Not only is it a wonderful garnish, it can be used as primary in soups and salads. It can be fried quickly in butter and poured over dishes served with browned butter, or deep-fried until crisp and used as a garnish for fried dishes.

**Rosemary** is derived from the leaves of a perennial, 5-foot high evergreen. The leaves are narrow and hard, have a strong but pleasant aroma, and are dried and used as a seasoning. Rosemary is excellent with lamb, and adds greatly to a salad dressing if used gently, and in stuffings. (Oddly, rosemary is also a moth repellant.)

**Saffron** is the dried stamens of the saffron (or safran) crocus, originating in the East. It was introduced into Spain by the Arabs, and has been cultivated in France since the sixteenth century. Saffron is picked carefully by hand, needing 70,000 or more stamens to make a pound. It is very expensive; an eighth teaspoon is worth over $22. The best saffron is dark orange in color without any white streaks. Sometimes it is faked with safflower—"bastard saffron"—which is more red in color. Dishes in which saffron is used are said to be "safrane."

**Savory** is a garden herb with a scent similar to thyme. There are two kinds: winter and summer. Both are strong and pungent; they should be applied sparingly. Summer savory is recommended mostly for sauces, egg, fish, and meat dishes. Winter savory, the stronger of the two, is used in frankfurters.

**Sesame** is a tropical and subtropical herbacious plant known to the Greeks, Hebrews, and Egyptians for centuries. The seeds are widely used in baking—breads, cookies, and cakes—and in confectionaries. They are also used for oil and "tahini"—sesame butter. Sesame seeds are a primary ingredient of homus, popular in much of the Middle East, and are used extensively by the Chinese.

**Soy sauce**, the most characteristic seasoning for Chinese food, is a dark, very salty liquid made from soy beans, salt, and water. Many kinds of soy sauce are produced in various regions of China and they differ in character as much as do beers brewed in various parts of the United States.

**Tamarind** is the fruit of the leguminous plant (pea and bean family) found in the West Indies. The pods are filled with an acid, juicy pulp used to prepare drinks like lemonade, citron cordials, orangeade, and the like, and sherbert. It can be used to replace vinegar.

**Thyme** is a small, shrubby plant and a member of the mint family. There are many kinds: golden, silver, woody, creeping moss, and on and on. (The English use thyme along the garden paths and when stepped on and crushed, gives off a delightful pungent fragrance.) Thyme is used to season meat and poultry dishes, as well as fish.

**Turmeric** is an East Indian root, a member of the ginger family. It is very hard, has to be ground, and has a sharp taste but is not hot. Turmeric is bright yellow, is a primary ingredient in curry, and is sometimes used alone to color foods.

# INDEX

# INDEX

# INDEX

# INDEX

# INDEX

# INDEX

## *ORDER FORM*

If you would like to order additional copies of *Dining in the Great Embassies* send:

$16.95 per copy plus $2.00 postage and handling to Peanut Butter Publishing. Washington State residents add 7.9% sales tax.

Please send me_____copies.

- - - - - - - - - - - - - - - - - - - - - - - - -

## BILL TO:

Name_____

Address_____

City_____State_____Zip_____

## SHIP TO:

Name_____

Address_____

City_____State_____Zip_____

Payment Enclosed ☐

Charge ☐

Visa # _____Exp. Date_____

MasterCard # _____Exp. Date_____

Signature _____

- - - - - - - - - - - - - - - - - - - - - - - - -

### PEANUT BUTTER PUBLISHING
329 2nd Avenue West, Seattle, WA 98119
1-800-426-5537    (206) 281-5965